NAMES OF CHRIST

NAMES OF CHRIST

T.C. HORTON
CHARLES E. HURLBURT

MOODY PRESS
CHICAGO

97-139

© 1994 by
THE MOODY BIBLE INSTITUTE
OF CHICAGO

Adapted from *The Wonderful Names of Our Wonderful Lord,*
written by T. C. Horton and Charles Hurlburt, originally pub-
lished in 1925.

ISBN: 0-8024-6040-2

1 3 5 7 9 10 8 6 4 2

Printed in the United States of America

To Paul Lentini,
friend and brother,
who names Christ "Yeshua."

ACKNOWLEDGMENTS

To Chris Criel,
for keying in the manuscript,
and to Cheryl Dunlop for copy editing.

INTRODUCTION

If someone asks what Christ means to you, how do you respond? The mystery of the Incarnation alone may leave us speechless; add to that Christ's words of life, powerful miracles, and mighty work of salvation through the cross, resurrection, and ascension into glory. Then we would need to describe the wonderful work of grace He performs inside us and in our circumstances. Our superlative phrases seem trite when trying to describe the reality of Jesus Christ. Sometimes we may feel safe simply describing Him as Saviour and Lord and not dealing with the complexities that go beyond our comprehension.

Yet the Person and Work of Christ is not just the territory of expert theologians. Jesus told the Pharisees to search the Scriptures in order to find *Him*. In fact, one of His names is "Word of God"—almost synonymous with the Bible itself.

In this regard, you will find hundreds of prophecies from the Old Testament describing the character and nature of the Messiah and His purpose in God's plan. We use these to prove that Jesus is the Christ. Yet there exists another resource in the Scriptures, largely overlooked, that will allow us to grasp at a deeper level the

Second Person of the Trinity in His full divinity and humanity. I am referring to the names of Christ, the title and subject matter of this volume. Though not considered as "important" as fulfilled prophecy, there is a hidden wealth of hundreds of names and word pictures describing the Word made Flesh which go beyond the more limiting functions of messianic prophecy.

When one contemplates the sheer beauty and variety of these names of Christ, the response is one of adoration and thanksgiving, especially as we realize He was all these things for *us*. The authors, T. C. Horton and Charles Hurlburt, have thus performed a great service in creating a devotional guide as opposed to an exegetical commentary. Certainly we would benefit from a linguistic treatment of the names of Christ as well. Yet we might miss the joy of deep communion with the God we are getting to know in ever greater depth as we call upon Him with names we rarely use. Moreover, the authors do often provide a context for each name to illumine its meaning in a given passage. This volume is a learning as well as a devotional experience.

Some of these names may surprise the reader because they are not traditionally associated with Christ. In fact, I removed some "names" because they reflected more of a function or action than the attributes of a person. One realizes, however, that the Person of Christ is present within the selections contained herein, even if in the Old Testament we may not always make the association. Arranged in scriptural order, one observes the "footprints" of Christ from the Fall in Genesis all the way to the heavenly city of Revelation.

These names vary greatly. The preincarnate Word is labeled "servant," only later to be known in His glorified state as "King of kings" for all eternity. I classify them (though not in the book) into three categories: (1) literal functions, such as prophet, priest, or king; (2) metaphorical functions, such as shepherd or bread of life; (3) poetic functions, to display an attribute symbolically, such as lily of the valley, or bright and morning star. The latter category stretches our imaginations as well as our intellects and hearts. Perhaps my favorite is the "Alpha and Omega" because it defines Jesus Christ as the reference point for all of time and eternity.

The added devotional feature is the prayers of various lengths by the authors and myself. This allows the reader to address the God who has revealed yet another facet of His character. Since the names originate from the King James Version, I have added alternative names from the New International Version for those unfamiliar with the KJV to dispel any resulting confusion. I have also edited the text and added a few names the authors inadvertently omitted, as well as making the aforementioned deletions.

As I've implicitly stated, the purpose is to view Christ in all His splendor, earthiness, and complexity. Here are some suggestions: Though this is not strictly a daily devotional, the reader could use the book daily into the autumn. Or because the text is short, half a dozen at a time could be read for prayer and meditation. Finally, more intense study into the nature of a name would yield fruit. The index at the back contains all the names listed in this volume, along with the Scripture references used in the text, to aid in that study. Using reference tools such as commentaries, concordances, and Bible dictionaries would be beneficial.

My primary hope is that you, the reader, grow in your knowledge and experience of Jesus Christ in order to be more like Him.

JAMES S. BELL, JR.

9

THE SEED OF THE WOMAN

And I will put enmity between thee and the woman, and between thy seed and her seed. *(Genesis 3:15)*

"Because He stooped so low God has exalted Him very high" (Philippians 2:9 Arthur Way's Translation). From this first great act and fact in His revelation to that last greater act when He died for our sins on Calvary, and up until the time when God exalted Him very high to sit at God's own right hand in the heavenlies, our Saviour's example was one of profound humility. He came from the bosom of the Father to become the "Seed of the Woman." The one who said, "the words which I have spoken to you, the same shall judge you," was, in His innocence, judged by sinful men and crucified.

Oh, You who humbled Yourself to be born of a woman, who bore our sins in Your own body on the tree, we bow on our faces before You and worship and adore You. May we empty ourselves to be filled by You. Amen.

Offspring of the woman - NIV

THE ANGEL OF THE LORD

And the Angel of the Lord called unto Abraham out of heaven the second time. *(Genesis 22:15)*

The "Angel (or Messenger) of Jehovah" was Himself God's message to us. He brought His own message to heal our deep sorrows and losses—He is our sin offering. He gave up His glory to bear our pain through the sacrifice of His own body on the cross.

We worship You, O "Angel of the Lord" and thank You that You are indeed a messenger for our salvation. Let us receive Your message with deep love and gratitude. Amen.

SHILOH (PEACEMAKER)

The sceptre shall not depart from Judah, nor a lawgiver from between his feet, until Shiloh come; and unto him shall the gathering of the people be. *(Genesis 49:10)*

Israel must walk in darkness under law until the years may seem eternity, but "Shiloh" comes at last and peace with Him. Has Shiloh come to you? And has the peace which passes understanding, the peace *He* made, entered into your soul? For Shiloh came and conquered every foe that could harass you, and He stands today offering the peace He made "that passes knowledge." Have you received it? Has Shiloh come in vain for you? Begin today and "in everything by prayer and supplication make your requests known to Him," and Shiloh's peace shall "calm your heart."

Lord, Your peace passes all our earthly understanding. Help us to remain obedient and faithful to You so that Your peace will remain. Amen.

THE STONE OF ISRAEL

But his bow abode in strength, and the arms of his hands were made strong by the hands of the mighty God of Jacob (from thence is the shepherd, the stone of Israel). *(Genesis 49:24)*

The "Stone of Israel," the chief Cornerstone, is rejected by the builders, a Stone of Stumbling, a Rock of Offense, a Foundation Stone, on which alone we build all that shall stand. He makes us a polished, living stone; built in with other stones; perhaps a pillar to stand permanently and always be a part of His temple, for His own indwelling.

Holy Lord, self-offered for my peace; through death that I might live, through fire that I might become indestructible—enlighten me today till I perceive Your peace that passes understanding. Amen.

The rock of Israel - NIV

12

THE PEACE OFFERING

> And if his oblation be a sacrifice of peace offering, he shall offer it without blemish before the Lord. *(Leviticus 3:1)*

Is there any point of dispute between your Lord and you? One little thing which you do not surrender? He is right. He cannot change. It is your heart which must surrender. Then can you receive the peace which passes knowledge. He has made the offering which these Old Testament sacrifices prefigured and which atones for all your past, but you must yield your will to Him. Shall it be now?

Lord Jesus, change my heart by Your power that I may know the wonderful blessings of peace with God through Your atoning blood. Amen.

Fellowship offering - NIV

A STAR

> I shall see him, but not now; I shall behold him, but not nigh: there shall come a Star out of Jacob, and a Sceptre shall rise out of Israel, and shall smite the corners of Moab, and destroy all the children of Sheth. *(Numbers 24:17)*

What could be more beautiful or more fitting than that our Lord should be called of God "a Star"? Those who know Him best may say, "I shall see Him, but not now. I shall behold Him, but not nigh." From far beyond our world of trouble and care and change, He shines with undimmed light, a radiant, guiding Star to all who will follow Him—a morning Star, a promise of a better day.

Lord God, Your star is a sign of hope, pointing to the heavens. Let us see You shining brightly as Maker of heaven and earth, and our personal Saviour. Amen.

A SCEPTRE

A Sceptre shall rise out of Israel. *(Numbers 24:17)*

There is a view of Jesus which men are slow to see, but some day all the world shall know that "a Scepter" shall rise out of Israel and evil will be destroyed before His righteousness more swiftly than ice must melt before the glowing sun. It is in the very nature of things that sin must be consumed before His glorious holiness. It can only be the love of sin that blinds the eyes of men to His consuming righteousness.

Search me, O God, and know my heart. Try me and know my thoughts, and see if there be any wicked way in me and lead me in the way everlasting. Then melt me, mold me, fill me, and use me. Amen.

THE CAPTAIN OF THE HOST OF THE LORD

And He said, Nay; but as captain of the host of the Lord am I now come. *(Joshua 5:14)*

The hosts of Israel stand before the gateway to a promised land. No swords are drawn, no skill have they, but with them is an unseen host, and with the host stands "the Captain of Jehovah's Host." Jericho and all the giants of the land submit, and for you, "behind the dim unknown stands God within the shadows keeping a watch above His own."

> Captain of the Hosts of God,
>   In the path where You have trod,
> Bows my soul in humble awe—
>   Take command. Your word is law.
>
> Cause me to possess the land,
>   Led by Your Almighty hand.
> Be my guide, defense and power,
>   Lead me from this very hour.

Lead me ever onward on the path of righteousness for Your name's sake. Amen.

THE ROCK OF MY SALVATION

> The Lord liveth; and blessed be my rock; and exalted be the God of the rock of my salvation. *(2 Samuel 22:47)*

No graver danger threatens the believer than that of forgetting that he was redeemed—forgetting even as he experiences it what our salvation cost, and who is the rock foundation of our faith. To meet this need our Saviour pictures Himself not merely as the Rock of Ages, and our Strong Rock of Refuge, but "the Rock of our Salvation." Here, in Him and based upon His merit and atoning grace, we were saved from among the lost. Let us glory in this precious name and never forget that He was "wounded for our transgressions" and that "He bore our sins in His own body on the tree."

Our precious Lord, may we have all joy and peace in believing that our salvation is built upon a solid Rock, standing through all ages. Amen.

The Rock, my Savior - NIV

THE LIGHT OF THE MORNING

> And he shall be as the light of the morning, when the sun riseth, even a morning without clouds. *(2 Samuel 23:4)*

No single name or picture of our Lord could possibly reveal Him as the full supply of all our need. Our Lord is to His people not only "the Morning Star," but when the lights of night shall fade in the dawning day, He becomes "the Light of the Morning." When all of earth's years have passed, when all earth's visions fade and flee away, when the great glory of that morning of our eternal life in heaven shall break upon us, we shall find that He who guided our entire earthly pilgrimage is still our source of life and guidance over there.

Lord God, precious Saviour, Your mercies are new every morning. May the bright star of Your love shine in our hearts, bringing joy at beginning of day. Amen.

THE DAYSMAN

Neither is there any daysman betwixt us, that might lay his hand upon us both. *(Job 9:33)*

When the day of reckoning comes, when by His just decrees I should hear the sentence which my sins deserve, when I shall stand before the Father, stripped of all pretense and sham, then will I fear no evil, for my "Daysman," Mediator, Arbitrator, will stand and speak for me. Can I do less than bow upon my face and worship Him, now and throughout eternity?

Jesus, You stand in the gap on my behalf, covering my sin. May no evil come between us, but only unbroken fellowship through the mediator of the covenant of grace. Amen.

Arbitrator - NIV

MY SHIELD

But thou, O Lord, art a shield for me; my glory, and the lifter up of mine head. *(Psalm 3:3)*

The storms of life assault us in many forms—demonic oppression, illness, financial worries, weaknesses of many kinds. But our great Shield protects us from them all. Just as at the cross, Christ stands in for us and is able to take the fierce onslaught of all evil, sin, and death.

O God, let us always and everywhere seek the covering of Your mighty Shield in order to remain strong. Amen.

MY GLORY

> But thou, O Lord, art a shield for me; my glory, and the lifter up of mine head. *(Psalm 3:3)*

That God is "glory"—or "excellence"—beyond our understanding, none can deny. But do our hearts look up to Him today in humble, earnest worship, and know the truth, and speak the truth—"You are *my Glory*"? Our safety lies in the fact that He possesses us. Our deepest, holiest joy comes only when we humbly say in the hour of secret worship, "You are mine."

O, Lord my Glory, be my shield this day. My head shall lift up to the heavens to Your majesty, and I shall hold my head high, because of Your mighty protection. Amen.

THE LIFTER UP OF MINE HEAD

> But thou, O Lord, art a shield for me; my glory, and the lifter up of mine head. *(Psalm 3:3)*

So often our heads are bowed down with worry, guilt, and shame. We should always look up and see the God who is "above" all our circumstances, working to reveal His glory on our behalf.

> Oh, You who have given
> Your glory to me,
> Anoint my blind eyes
> Till Your glory I see.
>
> Lift up my bowed head,
> Be my shield and my light,
> Till Your radiant glory
> Shall banish my night.

Lord Jesus, we often glory in earthly things. Put our eyes on things above, where You reign, to know the glory of heavenly things and await Your coming from heaven. Amen.

MY FORTRESS

> The Lord is my rock, and my fortress, and my deliverer; my God, my strength, in whom I will trust; my buckler, and the horn of my salvation, and my high tower. *(Psalm 18:2)*

"A mighty fortress is my God," and no evil may reach the soul that shelters there. There is no saint of God who may look back through all the troubled years of any earthly pilgrimage, and not say, if he shall speak truly, "I have been kept by the power of God." Every failure of our lives and each defeat has come when we have sought some earthly fortress rather than our Lord.

I am hiding, Lord, in You. Your walls are impregnable, so I can withstand life's onslaughts. Let our praise to You be as incense, O Lord. Amen.

MY SHEPHERD

> The Lord is my shepherd; I shall not want. *(Psalm 23:1)*

To say, "The Lord is *my Shepherd*," must carry with it in our understanding not merely grateful praise for the infinite grace and tenderness of the Great Shepherd who leads us by still waters and in green pastures, but confession of our own helplessness and need of a Shepherd's care. And a remembrance also of our lost, undone condition, until

> "All through the mountains, thunder-riven,
>   And up from the rocky steep,
> There arose a glad cry to the gates of heaven,
>   'Rejoice! I have found My sheep!'"

Lord Jesus, tender Shepherd, lead us forth this day in glad service for You. Feed, care for, and protect us from wolves and allow us to feed in Your green pastures. Amen.

RESTORER

> He restoreth my soul: he leadeth me in the paths of
> righteousness for his name's sake. *(Psalm 23:3)*

We wander from God and from the paths of righteousness—
from following Him beside the still waters—till we lose the
way, lose joy, lose the sound of His voice. Then the Master
"restores [the only use of this form in the Old Testament] our
soul"; "brings us back into His way," into the paths of righteousness.

*O, gracious "Restorer," bring back my wandering soul as
a straying sheep and lead me on in the paths of righteousness "for Your name's sake." Lead me in the everlasting way
as Your obedient servant. Amen.*

THE LORD MIGHTY IN BATTLE

> Who is this King of glory? The Lord strong and mighty, the
> Lord mighty in battle. *(Psalm 24:8)*

No life can be lived for God in these difficult days without terrific conflict. Foes within and foes without assail each saint
continuously. Principalities and powers are arrayed against
the child of God who seeks to serve his Master. We have no
might with which to meet "this great host that comes out
against us," but Jehovah, Mighty in Battle, is our Saviour, our
Intercessor, Our Elder Brother, our ever-present Friend.

*I must fight if I would win; increase my courage, Lord, and
save me from the massive array of foes. Protect me from all
evil and harm and fill me with Your Holy Spirit. Amen.*

KING OF GLORY

Who is this King of glory? The Lord of hosts, he is the King of glory. *(Psalm 24:10)*

Jehovah Jesus, the glorious King! Not merely *a* king, but glorious, excelling all others in mighty truth and power, grace and love. We almost forget for a time His absolute sovereignty as we bow in humble worship before His matchless glory, and cry again and again, "Thy kingdom come," O Glorious King.

Lord Jesus, let us open the gates of our heart so that the King of Glory might come in. You are our hope of glory. Prepare us to be glorified with You. Amen.

MY STRONG ROCK

Bow down thine ear to me; deliver me speedily: be thou my strong rock, for an house of defence to save me. *(Psalm 31:2)*

No sorrow of men is so deep and dark and bitter as to be without a refuge, a rock, a safe retreat. However deep our sorrow, however dark our sin, however hopeless our lot among men, the Man of Sorrows bore our sin in His own body on the tree. He carried all our grief. He is our "Strong Rock." A strong, safe house, in which I am defended from flesh, the world, the devil.

Lord, You are the rock on which we have our testimony. We shall not be moved because You are our solid foundation, a house no one can destroy. Amen.

Rock of refuge - NIV

A STRONG TOWER

For thou hast been a shelter for me, and a strong tower from the enemy. *(Psalm 61:3)*

What is the testimony of *our* souls today as we read that which others have said concerning Him who has been a "Strong Tower" from the enemy? Did any child of God in danger hasten within the Strong Tower of His Presence and find anything of failure or defeat? Must we not confess that every failure has come when we were found outside?

O Strong Tower, may we enter in today and dwell in You and be safe. What have we to fear with the safety of Your divine shelter all around us? Amen.

A STRANGER AND AN ALIEN

I am become a stranger unto my brethren, and an alien unto my mother's children. *(Psalm 69:8)*

He became an outcast for us so that we in turn could find our home with Him for all eternity. Let us identify with Him as aliens and strangers on this earth, for the One not received by His native land.

> What was the price He paid,
>   That, what he bore for me;
> "A STRANGER, AN ALIEN"; alone,
>   He died on Calvary.
>
> A "STRANGER" to make me a friend,
>   An "ALIEN" to give me a home.
> Great Stranger, I fall at Your feet,
>   No longer from You will I roam.

Lord Jesus, may we be strangers to the world in order to be friends with You who had no place to lay His head. Let us not love the world. Amen.

THE KING'S SON

> Give the king thy judgments, O God, and thy righteousness
> unto the King's Son. *(Psalm 72:1)*

How little do our hearts pay the homage due to God as K*ING*
and to Jesus as His S*ON*. We bow our heads, we lift our hats,
we pay our homage to the fleeting, trifling power of earth's
great men, but do we, as we enter the house of God, bow
humbly and revere *the King's Son?* Are earthly thoughts
hushed and earthly words stilled as we gather in the house of
God? Even when our worship leader voices our desires to
Him, do wandering thoughts of earthly things deprive us of
the blessing and the answer to our prayers?

Lord, teach us how to pray, that we may truly worship
You. Let us realize that it is to the Son of the Most High that
we speak. Draw us to Yourself and hear our imperfect
prayers that we may obtain mercy. Amen.

GOD'S FIRSTBORN

> Also I will make him my firstborn, higher than the kings of the
> earth. *(Psalm 89:27)*

"Remove your shoes from off your feet, for the place where
you stand is holy." The Eternal Father, God, is speaking. "My
Firstborn I will make higher than the kings of earth." You who
are the last-born of the Father, the Firstborn is your Elder
Brother. You have shared His humiliation leading to your salvation. You shall share His exaltation bringing you to your
eternal glory.

We worship You, Lord Jesus, God's "Firstborn"! We thank
You that we have been born again from the very life of the
Firstborn among many brethren. Amen.

THE HEAD STONE OF THE CORNER

> The stone which the builders refused is become the head
> stone of the corner. *(Psalm 118:22)*

Men may reject "The Head Stone of the Corner" and seek to
erect a building that shall stand, without the Living Christ. But
God has laid aside all human plans and made our Lord and
Saviour "The Head Stone of the Corner." When all human
buildings crumble and every earthly architect has failed, all
hearts bow before that perfect building, that eternal temple,
worshiping Him who is its crown of grace.

*You alone, Lord, can erect that building being joined to-
gether as the true house of God. Build each of us upon the
Chief Stone as a solid house of God.*

Capstone - NIV

MY HIGH TOWER

> My goodness, and my fortress; my high tower, and my
> deliverer; my shield, and he in whom I trust; who subdueth
> my people under me. *(Psalm 144:2)*

"My High Tower" is a vision of our glorious Saviour as the
Most High—high above our trials; high above our temptations; high above our foes; high above our failures and
losses; high above the fret and care of our earthward life. A
place of holy calm and peace and stillness. The door is open.

*Lord Jesus, our High Tower, let us enter in today. Only
then can we escape the defeat that will result from a lack of
Your protection. Let us look down from that High Tower on
our enemies and struggles. Amen.*

My stronghold - NIV

EXCELLENT

Let them praise the name of the Lord; for his name alone is excellent. *(Psalm 148:13)*

"All the glory of the Lord is that in which He excels all others." "His name is *Excellent,"* and all His names which represent some feature of His grace are glorious because they excel above any other name ever uttered among men. What friend, what helper do we know on earth that ever has or ever can approach His excellence? And so we turn with new deep joy to the psalmist's testimony, "They that know Your name shall put their trust in You."

Many may be called good, but You alone are excellent or perfect. Through Your grace we shall share in Your excellent benefits. We revere Your excellent name. Amen.

Exalted - NIV

A FRIEND THAT STICKS
CLOSER THAN A BROTHER

A man that hath friends must shew himself friendly: and there is a friend that sticks closer than a brother. *(Proverbs 18:24)*

Stay, lonely pilgrim, searching long for fellowship. Stop here and find "a Friend." "There *is* a Friend," though all the world deny it. One who is always true and faithful. One who never leaves and never forsakes. No brother will, or can, abide with us as He does. Will you be friend to Jesus, as He is friend to you?

We worship You, we trust all to You, and we take from You all peace, all grace, all needed power to do and be what pleases You, our never-absent Friend. You have called us friends rather than servants. May we live up to our calling. Amen.

OINTMENT POURED FORTH

Because of the savour of thy good ointments thy name is as ointment poured forth. *(Song of Solomon 1:3)*

Is your soul sore from sin, from chafing, or from the fiery darts of Satan, of sinners, or of saints? Then is your Lord to you as "Ointment Poured Forth," free, abundant, ready, healing and fragrant. Suffering soul, come near to Him and let that healing Ointment pour over you and soothe and heal you.

Lord Jesus, bind the wounds in our souls that are due to sin or injury. You alone can provide a soothing balm of healing and forgiveness to all our hurts. Amen.

Perfume poured out - NIV

BUNDLE OF MYRRH

A bundle of myrrh is my wellbeloved unto me. *(Song of Solomon 1:13)*

O, child of sorrow, sad soul suffocating in earth's dark vapors, your Lord is for you an exquisite perfume, "a Bundle of Myrrh." A missionary, wearily walking a winding pathway in the night, suddenly came upon a spot where the air was heavy with the perfume of wild jasmine and was comforted and refreshed by the fragrance preserved for a weary worker. So is your Lord to you a refreshing fragrance, "a bundle of myrrh."

Lord, Your mercy, love, and compassion are like the sweetest spices in our lives. Anoint us so we may be Your priests in worship. Amen.

Sachet of myrrh - NIV

CLUSTER OF CAMPHIRE

My beloved is unto me as a cluster of camphire in the vineyards of En-gedi. *(Song of Solomon 1:14)*

A beautiful, fragrant flower—"a cluster" of them—exquisite beauty, exquisite perfume in abundance! Struggling in the midst of experiences that are not fragrant, that are not delightful, have you learned to turn to Him, who, in the midst of darkness, is Light, in the midst of battle, is Peace, in the midst of unpleasantness, is to you unlimited and exquisite delight? Do you know your Lord as "a Cluster of Camphire"? Acquaint yourself with Him, and be at peace.

Lord, the beauty of Your holiness goes far beyond our senses. May the fragrance of Your presence fill our spiritual sense today and cause us to praise You ever more. Amen.

A cluster of henna blossoms - NIV

ROSE OF SHARON

I am the Rose of Sharon. *(Song of Solomon 2:1)*

Child of God, there is no circumstance of your life where Jesus fails to fit your need; to brighten as a brilliant rose your life. In joy or sorrow, sunshine or shadow, day or night, He blooms for you. Behold Him, then, today, not only on the Cross for you, not only on the Throne, but near you, close beside your path, "the Rose of Sharon."

Jesus our Lord, bloom in the barren places of our lives where we have not surrendered to You and cause the fragrance of Your love and healing to be known. Amen.

THE LILY OF THE VALLEYS

I am . . . the lily of the valleys. *(Song of Solomon 2:1)*

Sweetest, fairest, most exquisite flower that eye has seen, hidden except to eyes that seek it out. Your Lord unveils Himself to you in the same way, even though you walk through the valleys. Only in those deeper shadows can you know His utter loveliness. Behold Him then, and "fear no evil."

Lord, You reveal Yourself in all the beauties of nature. May Your grace and beauty permeate every area of our lives so that we may reflect Your loveliness. Amen.

HIM WHOM MY SOUL LOVETH

I will rise now, and go about the city in the streets, and in the broad ways I will seek him whom my soul loveth. *(Song of Solomon 3:2)*

We should seek the Lord along every twist and turn, every path on which He leads us in this life.

> Not in the doubting throng,
>   Not in the boastful song,
> But kneeling—with Christ above me—
>   Humbly I'll say, "I love Thee."
>
> Not with my lips alone,
>   Not for Your gifts I own,
> But just for the grace I see
>   Jesus, my soul loves Thee. Amen.

Lord, fill our souls with Your pure love so that we can truly call You our beloved and love You in return in word and deed. Amen.

The one my heart loves - NIV

THE CHIEFEST AMONG TEN THOUSAND

My beloved is white and ruddy, the chiefest among ten thousand. *(Song of Solomon 5:10)*

Do we sometimes sing with too little sincerity, "He's the Chiefest of Ten Thousand to my soul"? Is He really first in our hearts' affection? If so, His presence has been real to us, for He has said, "You shall seek Me and you shall find Me, when you search for Me with all your heart," or, "with your whole desire." Here the secret of full transforming communion with our Lord Jesus Christ is found in gazing upon Him in all the beauty of His holiness, until in actual truth He becomes in our hearts the "Chiefest of Ten Thousand."

Jesus Christ, may we desire You above the thousands of other temptations and distractions that this life presents. Only You provide true satisfaction and fulfillment. Amen.

Outstanding among ten thousand - NIV

ALTOGETHER LOVELY

His mouth is most sweet; yea, he is altogether lovely. *(Song of Solomon 5:16)*

There is no portion of our Lord Jesus Christ, His life or words, that is not perfect, pure, and beautiful.

> Every earthly joy will pall,
>   Every earthly friend will fall.
> Only Christ is to the end
>   "ALTOGETHER LOVELY," Friend.
>
> Do you see His wondrous face?
>   Full of glory, love and grace?
> Look and all your need confess,
>   Worship His pure Holiness.

Lord, it is difficult to see Your loveliness when we are marked with the ugliness of sin. Purify us in Your image to reflect Your beauty. Amen.

THE BRANCH OF THE LORD

> In that day shall the Branch of the Lord be beautiful and glorious. *(Isaiah 4:2)*

By every means and picture which we can understand the Spirit reveals our Saviour's oneness with God. None is more clear or full of meaning to us than this, "the Branch of the Lord." One with the Father, growing out of and yet a part of Him. And we are "branches" of Christ (see John 15). As we worship the Christ who is very God, we hear Him say, "If you abide in Me, you shall ask what you will, and it shall be done unto you."

Jesus, be a part of everything we do and say, and may Your life flow through us, making us one with You, as well as with the Father and Holy Spirit. Amen.

THE LORD OF HOSTS

> And one cried unto another, and said, Holy, holy, holy, is the Lord of hosts: the whole earth is full of his glory. *(Isaiah 6:3)*

The "Jehovah" (here, "Lord") of the Old Testament is the "Jesus" of the New. If we always think (as Scofield suggested) of Jehovah as "God revealing Himself," and the words of Jehovah-Jesus, "Blessed are the pure in heart for they shall see God," then shall the heavens about us be always full of the chariots and horsemen of the Lord of Hosts, and all fear shall be stilled and His revelation of Himself to us will not be in vain.

Lord Jesus, Jehovah of hosts, give us a vision of Your glory this day. May we experience Your omnipotent power and cry, "Holy holy," worshiping You this day. Amen.

The Lord Almighty - NIV

THE CHILD

> For before the child shall know to refuse the evil, and choose the good, the land that thou abhorrest shall be forsaken of both her kings. *(Isaiah 7:16)*

The first, last, and chief mark of Christ's Deity was His great humility. The greatest Sage and Seer of all the ages, "a child"! The Everlasting God, hoary-white with eternal years, "a child"! Shall we then hesitate to "become as little children," knowing that only so shall we enter the kingdom?

Lord, help us to become like little children with simple trust, purity of heart, and spontaneous love for the Child who became a man to die for us. Amen.

The boy - NIV

A SANCTUARY

> And he shall be for a sanctuary. *(Isaiah 8:14)*

Where is your place of worship? Where, in the turmoil of the street; where, in the busy cares of home; where, in the hurry and confusion of humanity, shall your soul find the place to pray? "He shall be for a 'Sanctuary,' closer to you than breathing, nearer than hands or feet." At any moment during all the hurried day you may be able to hide from earth's eyes, and in a quiet place from all earth's noise, just abide in Him.

Jesus Christ, let us retreat into the sacred place, for You are right here now, closer than our breath and yet interceding with the Father. We love You, Lord. Amen.

A GREAT LIGHT

The people that walked in darkness have seen a great light:
they that dwell in the land of the shadow of death, upon them
hath the light shined. *(Isaiah 9:2)*

It is the people who once walked in darkness who are able to
see the greatness of the light. It is the soul which finds it is
lost that seeks the Lord. Have you seen the Light? The beloved apostle said, "That which we have seen and heard declare we unto you. . . . This then is the message which we
have heard of him, and declare unto you, that God is light,
and in him is no darkness at all."

*Lord, let my life and lips tell out the story of the Light my
eyes have seen. Let the brightness of Your radiance lead me
in Your path, out of the way of death. Amen.*

WONDERFUL

For unto us a child is born, unto us a son is given . . . his
name shall be called Wonderful. *(Isaiah 9:6)*

Jesus is "the same yesterday, today, and forever," and men
who think Him commonplace or at most only an unusual
man, will someday stand ashamed and overwhelmed as they
hear this prophecy fulfilled: "His name shall be called *Wonderful.*" Today He is working just as wonderful works as He
performed when He created the heaven and the earth. His
wondrous grace, His wonderful omnipotence, is for His child
who needs Him and who trusts Him, even today. Attempt
great things for God and expect great things from Him and
you will begin even now to say, His name is Wonderful.

*Truly, Lord, Your Person and Works make us full of won-
der. Let us bow before You and contemplate Your awesome
attributes. Amen.*

COUNSELLOR

> For unto us a child is born . . . and his name shall be
> called . . . Counsellor. *(Isaiah 9:6)*

Not often is He called "Counsellor" now. Even God's saints
continuously ask men instead of God, "How may I find God's
will?" Conference after conference is held by both the world
and the church to find by human wisdom some better plan
for earthly government, or for the church, or for the welfare of
our earthly life and walk. But how rarely do we bow together
or alone to seek that heavenly wisdom, that divine counsel,
which alone will enable us to find our way out of the mazes
in which we wander. When shall His name be joyfully and tri-
umphantly proclaimed as "Counsellor" by His people? By
you?

*Lord Jesus, give us wise counsel in all the decisions and
challenges we face today, and grant us wisdom and direc-
tion to do Your will. Amen.*

THE MIGHTY GOD

> For unto us a child is born, unto us a son is given; . . . and his
> name shall be called . . . the mighty God. *(Isaiah 9:6)*

Have we doubted His might and feared, in the day when
some foe was near? His name is "The Mighty God." Do away
with all doubt and fear! "You have made both the heaven and
earth. There is nothing too hard for You."

*Lord, I bow to the dust and worship. Mighty God, show
Your power in me! For Your might is made perfect in my
weakness and You have promised to do this very thing.
Amen.*

THE EVERLASTING FATHER

For unto us a child is born, unto us a son is given . . . and his name shall be called . . . the everlasting Father. *(Isaiah 9:6)*

Who has mourned a father's death and felt the loss of his temporary power and helpfulness? The Child who was born in Bethlehem, who gave His life for you, is not alone your Saviour and your King, but "His name shall be called *the Everlasting Father.*" In His everlasting love, within His everlasting arms, within His Father-heart which has mercy on you, His child, you shall find safety, rest, and comfort.

Dear God, we thank You for the never-ending love You have for Your children. We marvel how the Child Jesus Christ can also be known as our Everlasting Father. Amen.

THE PRINCE OF PEACE

For unto us a child is born, unto us a son is given . . . and his name shall be called . . . the Prince of Peace. *(Isaiah 9:6)*

He who proclaimed to loyal hearts, "Peace I leave with you, my peace I give unto you: not as the world giveth give I unto you," is rightly called "the Prince of Peace." He who brought such peace to earth was rejected by men and still waits to be crowned on earth; but He gives before that royal day a peace that passes understanding to every trusting heart. Have you received it? Will you, in loyalty to "the Prince of Peace," accept in humble faith His peace today?

We thank You, mighty Prince, that You who came to do battle with the enemy of our souls have made peace between us and the Father. May Your peace rest deeply in our hearts. Amen.

THE LIGHT OF ISRAEL

> And the light of Israel shall be for a fire, and his Holy One for a flame; and it shall burn and devour his thorns and his briers in one day. *(Isaiah 10:17)*

Jesus was and is the "Light of Israel." He is also the "Light of Life" and the "Light of men," a "Light to lighten the world." But the "Light of Israel" was "to burn and devour thorns and briers." Dear child of God, are you bringing the useless branches, the unpleasant, unlovely things of your life into the Light of His Presence that they may be consumed? Some day the shining of His presence will destroy the very advocate of evil. Shall we not submit our lives to that Wondrous Light and ask Him to consume all evil in us?

O Lord, Your presence is both light and fire within us. May it burn ever more brightly and create a clear reflection of Your majesty. Amen.

A ROD OUT OF THE STEM OF JESSE

> And there shall come forth a rod out of the stem of Jesse, and a Branch shall grow out of his roots. *(Isaiah 11:1)*

Only a "rod" from a human "stem"? Only a "root" from "dry ground"? Has he no "form nor comeliness," no beauty that we should desire? "Surely He bore our griefs" and the way of "our peace" was in Him. "Because He stooped so low God has exalted Him very high," and the beauty of this tender plant was the glory of God on high.

O Lord, by Your rod, rule and correct us in order that through loving discipline we shall be fit to enter Your kingdom. Amen.

A shoot out of the stump of Jesse - NIV

A BRANCH OUT OF JESSE'S ROOTS

A Branch shall grow out of his roots. *(Isaiah 11:1)*

Of all the miracles that attest to the deity of our Lord, including the miraculous preservation of the Scriptures, none is more wonderful or convincing to the honest, faithful heart than the preservation, not only of Israel, but of that section of Israel, humble in its origin, which revealed our Lord to be born of the family of David and of Jesse. Out of the nations scattered over the earth, out of the line of kings who long had ceased to reign, there came forth, as the prophet said, a "Branch out of the Roots" of the stem of Jesse. And He who was of the seed of David shall just as surely come again to reign once more over Israel, and through Israel over all the earth.

Lord, our faint hearts believe anew in God's eternal truth and faithfulness. Preserve us as a remnant to serve You and further Your kingdom. Amen.

A Branch will bear fruit - NIV

A ROOT OF JESSE

And in that day there shall be a root of Jesse . . . to it shall the Gentiles seek: and his rest shall be glorious. *(Isaiah 11:10)*

It is not Israel alone who shall rejoice when a root of Jesse shall stand for a sign of the people, for "to it shall the Gentiles seek," and all the gracious promises and gifts God gave to Jesse and to David and his seed which could bring rest and comfort to our souls belong to us who worship Jesus, David's Son and Jesse's Root. How all the grace and glory of our God through all the ages is gathered up for us who from the Gentile world bow at His feet and find His glorious rest!

Lord Jesus, thank You for the Father's plan to provide a Messiah from a long line of righteous men. May we the church continue Your lineage and live up to our calling. Amen.

35

AN ENSIGN OF THE PEOPLE

> And in that day there shall be a root of Jesse, which shall stand for an Ensign of the people; to it shall the Gentiles seek: and his rest shall be glorious. *(Isaiah 11:10)*

Jesus is the people's flag, an "Ensign of the People." Wherever and whenever He is lifted up, the people seek after Him. Is not our failure to win many to the Lord due to our misrepresentation of Him? To our failure to reveal the beauty of His holiness and to enter into His glorious rest? Shall we bow in humble confession while we pray that we who are His representatives may not misrepresent Him by lives that are unlike His. Let us seek for grace to exalt Him everywhere among the unsaved.

Lord God, Your banner over us is love. Let us live under the standard of Your holiness and wear Your colors proudly as we witness for You. Amen.

A banner for the peoples - NIV

JEHOVAH

> Behold, God is my salvation; I will trust, and not be afraid: for the Lord JEHOVAH is my strength and my song; he also is become my salvation. *(Isaiah 12:2)*

Jehovah—"The self-existent One who reveals Himself." Into the wilderness of my lost way He comes to find me and lead me out. Into the desert of my barren life enters Jehovah and makes all the desert a garden. Into my death He brings His life and to my dead senses reveals Himself the One Eternal God. Shall we not bow before His Majesty and worship Jehovah, while we pray for greater grace to receive all the revelation of Himself which He would give?

O Lord, may we prepare Your way in a dry and barren land, making Your path clear to all. You are the Way, Truth, and Life. Amen.

Lord - NIV

MY STRENGTH AND MY SONG

> Behold, God is my salvation; I will trust, and not be afraid: for the Lord JEHOVAH is my strength and my song; he also is become my salvation. *(Isaiah 12:2)*

We know Jehovah is our "Strength," but do we make Him also our "Song"? As we make Him so and sing of Him, we lose our fear. We are able to "trust and not be afraid" only as we sing of Him. Our Redeemer is our "strength." Make Him also your "song" today.

Our great stronghold, may You become our joyous song today, full of praise of Your name. We shall sing of Jehovah, our great strength in time of need. Amen.

A NAIL IN A SURE PLACE

> And I will fasten him as a nail in a sure place; and he shall be for a glorious throne to his father's house. *(Isaiah 22:23)*

We may have many imaginative notions concerning Christ as a "Nail in a Sure Place." Whatever else this name may or may not mean, it brings to the worshiping child of God a sense of the fixedness, the certainty and security of Jesus Christ in His relationship to the temple and throne of God. If we on earth are being built together as a house for God, yet more certain still is the fact of the presence of Christ filling the house. If we are pillars who remain, it is because He is secure—His place is "fastened" and "sure." "So shall we be ever with the Lord," for where He is, there shall also His servants be, and our abiding there is as sure as Christ's.

Lord, You hold all things together by the word of Your power. Fasten us to Yourself so we cannot be separate from You. Nail our hearts to Yours. Amen.

A peg into a firm place - NIV

37

A GLORIOUS THRONE

> And he shall be for a glorious throne to his father's house.
> *(Isaiah 22:23)*

One of the most vivid pictures painted by the Holy Spirit of the life that lies beyond occurs in Revelation—the swift, wondrous vision of the church on earth (Revelation 4:2–3). "Behold a throne was set in Heaven . . . and there was a rainbow round about the throne." That rainbow brings us hope and comfort and the precious, glorious promise that our Lord Himself is a "Glorious Throne to His Father's House." Let it be no longer hard or difficult for you to pray. The throne before which you bow is not one of austere justice but rather one of infinite grace. Let us therefore come boldly to the throne of grace, that we may obtain mercy and find help.

Jesus Christ, seated at the right hand of the Father, intercede from the place of glorious beauty—Your throne in heaven—where we will reign with You for all eternity. Amen.

A seat of honor - NIV

STRENGTH TO THE POOR

> For thou hast been a strength to the poor, a strength to the needy in his distress. *(Isaiah 25:4)*

Touched with a feeling of our infirmities our Lord in His omnipotence becomes a "Strength to the Poor and Needy." Let us never forget that His strength is made perfect in our weakness only when we realize our helplessness and fling ourselves, as trusting children, into the outstretched arms by which He "created the heavens and the earth." With what wondrous picture does our Lord reveal Himself as the supply for our every need and "strength to the poor"!

Lord, apart from You we are poor, weak, blind, and naked. Clothe, feed, and strengthen us with Your mighty supply. Amen.

Refuge for the poor - NIV

A SHADOW FROM THE HEAT

For thou hast been . . . a shadow from the heat. *(Isaiah 25:4)*

In the intolerable heat of the sun as it beats upon the plateaus of equatorial Africa, one may step from the unbearable heat to a shade so cool, so refreshing, that until it is experienced it is almost beyond conception or belief. Thus our Lord pictures Himself to His weary, toiling children, struggling onward in the heat of almost impossible experiences, as a "Shadow from the Heat," into whose presence we may step at any moment of our pilgrimage and find cool, refreshing rest.

Dear Lord Jesus, the heat of our toil and trouble makes us weary. Let the cool shade of Your presence refresh us and help us persevere. Amen.

A shade from the heat - NIV

A REFUGE FROM THE STORM

For thou hast been . . . a refuge from the storm . . . when the blast of the terrible ones is as a storm against the wall. *(Isaiah 25:4)*

"God is faithful, who will not suffer you to be tempted above that ye are able, but will with the temptation also make a way to escape"—a "refuge from the storm"—"that ye may be able to bear it." It is necessary for us to pass through storms and to feel their force and chilling blast, for only in such experiences could we ever know the comfort, the witness, of Him who is our "Refuge from the Storm." Are we hiding in Him?

Lord, help us to be able to bear all the storms of this life because no matter what happens, You are our refuge. Provide the escape in every danger, we pray, Deliverer. Amen.

A shelter from the storm - NIV

EVERLASTING STRENGTH

Trust ye in the Lord for ever: for in the Lord is everlasting strength. *(Isaiah 26:4)*

Many of the college buildings at Oxford University, hundreds of years old, were described by one who studied there more than half a century ago as "leprous with age." Many are crumbling away, and some must be replaced to save the buildings. The strongest rocks in which men bury the bodies of departed friends are oftentimes split apart by a growing plant. But He who calls us to "trust in Jehovah forever" calls Himself "An Everlasting Rock" or "The Rock of Ages." Let us trust in Him today, tomorrow, and forever.

Lord Jesus, there is neither spot nor wrinkle in You. You are solid, pure, and eternal. Help us to abide in You. Amen.

The Rock eternal - NIV

A CROWN OF GLORY

In that day shall the Lord of hosts be for a crown of glory . . . unto the residue of his people. *(Isaiah 28:5)*

We hear and think much of redeemed and fruitful saints shining as stars in the crown of our Lord, but in this wondrous title of our glorious Saviour we have a new vision of His relationship to His people. Souls who have been downtrodden and scorned by those whom the world calls great will in that day find that the King of Glory will be to them in the eyes of all a witness, a "Crown of Glory." Oh, you who are redeemed from among the lost, you who were dead and are now alive, were lost and are found, behold His wondrous grace!

Lord God, may we be willing to carry the cross in order to wear the crown. May we each become a bright jewel in Your diadem, so that we, like You, will shine like the sun. Amen.

A glorious crown - NIV

A DIADEM OF BEAUTY

> In that day shall the Lord of hosts be for a crown of glory, and
> for a diadem of beauty, unto the residue of his people.
> *(Isaiah 28:5)*

The difference between a Crown of Glory and a Diadem of
Beauty is that in the first the excellence, the worth, the value,
the glory of God shall be upon the saints. In the other, the
beauty, the very radiance of the Lord, shall fill and shine out
from those who, in a moment, in the twinkling of an eye,
shall be changed into His likeness. Oh, humble child of God,
see the exceeding grace which shall be revealed in the ages
to come. The beauty of the Lord our God shall be upon you,
and He shall be a crown or "Diadem of Beauty" to you. "He
that has this hope in Him purifies himself."

*Lord, it is awesome to imagine sharing Your personal
beauty. Thank You that Your beauty, which is imperfection in
us now, will shine perfectly one day. Amen.*

A beautiful wreath - NIV

A SURE FOUNDATION

> Therefore thus saith the Lord God, Behold, I lay in Zion . . . a
> sure foundation. *(Isaiah 28:16)*

All the chiseling, all the polishing of experiences through
which we pass, is costly. Will it last? Is it worthwhile? Worthwhile to suffer on and say, "Dear Lord, do not hold back Your
hand to comfort us and steady us." Through just such testing
times the Master calls Himself a "Sure Foundation." No ex-
periment here, no doubt, no room for anxious thought or
fear. He who builds upon that "Sure Foundation" finds his
building sure, and he shall be a pillar in the temple of God.

*Lord, there is no other foundation upon which our faith
can be built, and Your promises are effective in the midst of
trial. Thank You, God. Amen.*

A TRIED STONE

Therefore thus saith the Lord God, Behold, I lay in Zion for a foundation a stone, a tried stone, a precious corner stone. *(Isaiah 28:16)*

How strange is this experience of our Lord. Surely the Father knew the Son, knew His every capability and power. Yet He was tried by God as we need to be tried, to leave us an "example that we might walk in His steps." What mockery, what blasphemy, that He should be rejected by some builders of their own lives! Let us ask the great Master Builder to try us and chisel us until we fit in the place He has prepared for us.

Lord Jesus, You have passed the test of faithfulness. Make us solid stones through Your grace and power. Amen.

A tested stone - NIV

A HIDING PLACE FROM THE WIND

And a man shall be as an hiding place from the wind. *(Isaiah 32:2)*

Standing one day on the deck of a ship in the harbor at Aden, a traveler saw a storm of wind sweeping across the desert like some high, mountainous wave, rolling and sweeping forward until it struck the sea and lashed it to foam. Then it went on across the bay until it struck the ships lying there at anchor, till nearly every boat was torn from its moorings or forced to loosen every cable and steam with full force into the face of the terrific wind. There was no hiding place. In the same way, the storms of hate, of evil, and of sin sweep over our lives as we journey toward our everlasting home. But for every soul who knows his own helplessness, our Saviour is Himself a "Hiding Place from the Wind."

Our great God, the winds of temptation and adversity grow strong. Put us in a safe, calm place to experience Your grace and strength. Amen.

A shelter from the wind - NIV

SHADOW OF A GREAT ROCK IN A WEARY LAND

And a man shall be as . . . the shadow of a great rock in a
weary land. *(Isaiah 32:2)*

Journeying one night in the wilderness of central Africa in a
section plagued by many ravenous beasts, we found no place
of safety till we came to the shadow of a great rock, where we
sat down with our backs to the rock. We built a large fire at
our feet and there found rest and refreshment for the next
day's still weary journey. O, weary child, when your strength
fails and you can go no further, sit down and lean back in the
shadow of your Lord, upon Him. There build in prayer the fire
of faith and find rest and refreshment for your onward march.

*Hide us, our Lord, in the clefts of the Rock that is "higher
than I." May nothing shake or stand in the way of your rock-
like presence in our lives. Amen.*

RIVERS OF WATER IN A DRY PLACE

And a man shall be as . . . rivers of water in a dry place.
(Isaiah 32:2)

To know the blessing of water in abundance we need to have
felt a very keen thirst. Wandering one time in part of Africa's
desert, two missionaries traveled without water until thirst
became first a pain, then an agony, then almost insanity. After long marching over dry, burning sands they came to the
waters of a wide, deep river and quenched their thirst. "If any
man thirst let him come unto Me," and He is near. No matter
how deep our thirst, how great our longing or our need, He
who is as "Rivers of Water in a Dry Place" has said, "Lo, I am
with you. Drink and be satisfied."

*Our Saviour, we cannot live without the waters of life.
May our spirits be nourished with living water gushing up to
eternal life. Amen.*
Streams of water in the desert - NIV

43

THE KING IN HIS BEAUTY

> Thine eyes shall see the king in his beauty: they shall behold
> the land that is very far off. *(Isaiah 33:17)*

"Blessed are the pure in heart: for they shall see God." Do our
lives see the King in His beauty? Do we grasp the fact that as
we gaze upon Him it is His will that we should be changed
into the same likeness, "from glory to glory"? "A little while
and the world sees Me no more, but you see Me." No more
wonderful promise is ours for present experiences than this.
O Lord, let every mist and veil that hide Your glory, and every
sin, be put away, that we may behold You in the beauty of holiness. Then "the beauty of the Lord your God shall be upon
you."

*Lord, may we contemplate Your beauty in the Word, in na-
ture, and as You are revealed in others. May we reflect a
glimmer of that beauty as well. Amen.*

OUR LAWGIVER

> For the Lord is our judge, the Lord is our lawgiver, the Lord is
> our king; he will save us. *(Isaiah 33:22)*

Every nation, every act, every life, needs a law to direct it in its
relation to its own expression, and to others. That law must
be made by one who knows and understands the nation, act,
or life. Jesus is our "Lawgiver." He who gave us life, He who
has lived the life we need to live—He knows. He made the
law for us in infinite tenderness and love. "He that hath my
commandments and keepeth them, he it is that loveth me."

*Lord Jesus, as the psalmist exclaims, "I love Your law."
May it be a light to our path and a lamp to our feet. Through
obedience may we please You in everything. Amen.*

44

THE LORD GOD

> Behold, the Lord God will come with strong hand, and his arm shall rule for him: behold, his reward is with him, and his work before him. *(Isaiah 40:10)*

Not every soul that worships Jehovah has learned that the secret of all power and of fullness of blessing is in making Him the Master of our lives. Adonai Jehovah ("the Lord God") is the Lord, the Ruler, the Master, who in eternal grace reveals Himself. Shall we not humbly bow at His feet and crown Him Lord, Master, of all that we have and are?

Jesus, You are the great I Am, One with the Father. May we never forget Your transcendence as well as the fact that You are God with us. Amen.

The Sovereign Lord - NIV

THE EVERLASTING GOD

> Hast thou not known? hast thou not heard, that the everlasting God, the Lord, the Creator of the ends of the earth, fainteth not, neither is weary? there is no searching of his understanding. *(Isaiah 40:28)*

Jesus Christ and the Father work continually on our behalf to complete the good work they started until the day of salvation.

> Everlasting, never-ending
> Age-abiding is my Lord.
> Never shadow caused by turning,
> Changeless, perfect, is His Word.
>
> Everlasting God, I pray You
> Steady, strengthen, stablish me.
> Safe from grief and pain and failure,
> Hide me, Everlasting God, in Thee.

Everlasting and Infinite God, You are the same from before the beginning of time. Work mightily in our lives to secure our glorious future with You. Amen.

GOD'S ELECT

> Behold my servant, whom I uphold, mine elect, in whom my
> soul delighteth; I have put my spirit upon him; he shall bring
> forth judgment to the Gentiles. *(Isaiah 42:1)*

The infinite God, who knows and understands, the God of
wisdom and of knowledge, called in review all angels and all
men of all the ages and of all time and chose our Lord and
called Him "elect," to be the world's Redeemer, Saviour,
Friend, and the believer's All in All. Does your choice fall on
Him, each day, each hour, in each experience? May He be all
in all to you today.

*Lord Jesus, You were chosen for the greatest mission of
all time—winning our salvation. Thank You so much—that
we too are elected and have the unsurpassed privilege of being Your children. Amen.*

My chosen one - NIV

A LIGHT OF THE GENTILES

> I the Lord have called thee in righteousness, and will . . . give
> thee . . . for a light of the Gentiles. *(Isaiah 42:6)*

"In him was life, and the life was the Light of men." But how
shall that Light lighten the Gentiles unless we who are the
light of the world shall go forth among the Gentiles and let
the light shine? Someone brought that Light to us. Shall we
not bear it on a little farther into the darkness of some other
life? He *is* the Light. He *gave* the Light. *We* are the *Light-
bearers.*

*Lord Jesus, without Your Light we could never understand
God. Thank You for bringing Your truth to the Gentiles and
grafting us into Your Body. Let Your light now shine through
us. Amen.*

A POLISHED SHAFT

> And he hath made my mouth like a sharp sword; in the shadow of his hand hath He hid me, and made me a polished shaft. *(Isaiah 49:2)*

Our Lord is pictured as the "Word of God" having a "voice as the sound of many waters," and speaking to His people words of peace, comfort, and power. When He speaks and His word cuts through our selfish lives like a sword of radiant light, let us rejoice. Few human friends are faithful, but He who is "A Polished Shaft" speaks not only with eternal love but with unchanging faithfulness.

Speak, Lord, for Your servant hears You. Let Your sharp sword probe and eliminate those areas deep within that are not pleasing in Your sight. Let Your shaft bring healing to our innermost parts, to attain godliness. Amen.

A polished arrow - NIV

THE HOLY ONE OF ISRAEL

> Thus saith the Lord, the Redeemer of Israel . . . Kings shall see and arise, princes also shall worship, because of the Lord that is faithful, and the Holy One of Israel, and he shall choose thee. *(Isaiah 49:7)*

All Israel walked in sin. All Israel was defiled. And yet in cloud by day, in fire by night, within the holy tabernacle there stood a Presence, holy, infinite in love and grace and power. "The Holy One of Israel" could not forget His chosen people nor resist their faintest cry. So Israel stood and lived, and lives today because "The Holy One of Israel" stood beside them. And beside your soul He stands today to be your righteousness and lead you to Himself. Behold Him and adore!

Lord God, we adore You for You are completely holy and You long to bring this perfection to us. Thank You that we are the objects of Your love. Amen.

A ROOT OUT OF A DRY GROUND

> For he shall grow up before him as a tender plant, and as a root out of a dry ground. *(Isaiah 53:2)*

Dear discouraged soul, does it seem sometimes to you that your lot is a hard one? That you have been asked to stand in difficult places and where surrounding conditions have been most unfavorable? He who redeemed you knows every difficulty, every sorrow, which you can feel. He has suffered "in all points like we" and is, therefore, able to aid us. Then consider Him who grew up "A Root Out of a Dry Ground," or you will grow weary and faint with all that you face.

Lord God, please water the dry places in our lives and help us to remain rooted in Your sustaining love. Amen.

A MAN OF SORROWS

> He is despised and rejected of men; a man of sorrows, and acquainted with grief; and we hid as it were our faces from him; he was despised and we esteemed him not. *(Isaiah 53:3)*

He who was the source of all joy, the giver of all peace, He before whom angels and archangels bow in adoration, is also called a Man of Sorrows. Grief broke His heart, crushed out His life. Shall we through disobedience, rebellion, or lack of love or service or worship, add to the sorrows which He bore? Shall we murmur if we too shall be permitted to partake of His sorrows or to share His grief? He sorrowed all alone, except perhaps as angels ministered to Him in Gethsemane's deep shadow. But He shares your grief, He carries all your sorrow and comforts those who trust in Him. Shall we not worship and adore the "Man of Sorrows"?

O Suffering Servant, Your sorrows have brought us joy. Yet we pray that You would also bear the light sorrow and pain of this present life that come from our fallen nature. Amen.

GOD'S RIGHTEOUS SERVANT

> He shall see of the travail of his soul, and shall be satisfied:
> by his knowledge shall my righteous servant justify many; for
> he shall bear their iniquities. *(Isaiah 53:11)*

There are many servants, but only *One* is righteous. Paul was
able to say, "I have declared unto you the whole counsel of
God, I have fought a good fight, I have kept the faith," but still
he must call himself an unprofitable servant and less than the
least of all saints. Shall we therefore become discouraged
and conclude that it is not worthwhile to try? No, "your labor
is not in vain in the Lord," for He who was God's *righteous
servant* shall justify many. He is still "Jehovah Tsidkenu,"
(our Righteousness), and we may bring the dropped stitches
of our best weaving and the broken efforts of our best service,
and laying all at His feet rejoice that we are justified by Him
who is "God's Righteous Servant."

*Jesus Christ, we are so grateful to acquire Your righteous-
ness by Your work and our response of faith. Thank You for
choosing and justifying us before the Father. Amen.*

MY MAKER

> For thy Maker is thine husband. *(Isaiah 54:5)*

We hear of "self-made people," of people who are made by
their surroundings, or by devoted friends and fellows. How
rarely do we hear today the humble, joyful boast, "By the
grace of God I am what I am." And yet "He is your Maker"! All
you are that is lasting, all you are that is good, all you are that
is helpful, God has made. Bow then before your Maker. Worship and petition Him to finish that which He began.

*Creator God, our entire being and all our circumstances
originate from You. Bring us humility, diligence, and grateful-
ness as we acknowledge You as Author of all that is. Amen.*

MY HUSBAND

For thy Maker is thine husband. *(Isaiah 54:5)*

The bridegroom waits for the perfecting of His bride, yet even now we are joined together in inseparable union with Christ, who not only made us but is our betrothed.

Jesus, we seek an intimate union with You by allowing You to be our Head in all things, as we submit to You. Amen.

THE GOD OF THE WHOLE EARTH

The Lord of hosts is his name; and thy Redeemer the Holy One of Israel; the God of the whole earth shall he be called. *(Isaiah 54:5)*

Is there any part of the earth that is mine? Not till I am truly a child of "The God of the Whole Earth." May I not receive Him and possess all things in Christ and proceed to enjoy them, untroubled by the world's woe? Not till the whole earth has heard that He is "the God," not of a few, but "of the whole earth."

The cattle on a thousand hills belong to You, O Lord, as well as everything we own. Thank You that all things are ours and we will inherit a new heaven and earth. May we surrender everything to You for Your divine use. Amen.

A WITNESS TO THE PEOPLE

> Behold, I have given him for a witness to the people, a leader and commander to the people. *(Isaiah 55:4)*

A witness of the love of God, the grace, the power, the holiness of deity. No flaw in all that matchless testimony, no doubtful, double-meaning speech. He could say, "He that has seen Me has seen the Father." We too are witnesses, but oh, how full of flaws is all our testimony! The Father dwelt with Him and He sought the Father's guidance at every step and every word. We too may see and hear and walk with God, and so alone shall our witness win the wanderers home.

God of all truth, let us never fail to testify as Jesus did to the reality and love of the Father in heaven. Let us rely on Your guidance and strength to make us witnesses in Your Spirit. Amen.

A LEADER

> Behold, I have given him for a witness to the people, a leader and commander to the people. *(Isaiah 55:4)*

From the beginning of our Christian lives the fact that "He leads me" is one of the most blessed thoughts that comes to a child of God. But we think most often of His leading to battle, leading out of the mazes of confusion and ignorance, leading through the darkness of our night. Do we realize the infinite tenderness that makes Him gently lead those who are doing the finest and most difficult and unknown service of the world? The sorrow, the loneliness, the pain, which no friend on earth can know, He understands, He feels with us; and He gently leads us through the shadows to His own great glory. Shall we not follow where He leads and keep so close to Him that we shall never miss the way?

Lord Jesus, help us to be faithful followers of You, the one who leads us to eternal life. Amen.

A COMMANDER

> Behold, I have given him for a witness to the people, a leader and commander to the people. *(Isaiah 55:4)*

In a day when nearly everyone desires to do that which is right in his own eyes, it becomes difficult for all God's children to recognize His right to command. Yet He who redeemed us, who bought us so that we are not our own, proclaimed His right to the title of "Commander." Failure to obey will account for most of the loss of communion and joy in prayer and in the study of God's Word. If there be any commandment which He has brought home to our hearts which we have not obeyed, shall we not today grant Him instant, cheerful, loving obedience, and make Him in every detail of life our *Commander?*

Lord, Your commands are not burdensome to us. Bring understanding and obedience through the works You would have us do to build Your kingdom. Amen.

THE REDEEMER

> And the Redeemer shall come to Zion, and unto them that turn from transgression in Jacob, saith the Lord. *(Isaiah 59:20)*

When failure comes and disappointment, when your soul has been defeated and the race seems hopeless, stop and think "your Lord redeemed you and at countless cost." If He saw in you something worth dying for, giving Himself, His all, is it not worthwhile to rise and try again, walking with Him and worshiping Him who redeemed you?

Lord Christ, You have purchased us at a very great price and for an exalted purpose. Help us to redeem the time for Your glory, because the days are evil. Amen.

EVERLASTING LIGHT

Thy sun shall no more go down; neither shall thy moon withdraw itself; for the Lord shall be thine everlasting light, and the days of thy mourning shall be ended. *(Isaiah 60:20)*

No picture is more difficult for us to apprehend spiritually than a time when the sun shall no more go down, when Christ shall be to us "Everlasting Light." Our lives are so filled with ups and downs, with lights and shadows, that stability seems almost inconceivable and everlasting darkness easier to understand than everlasting light. Yet this is what Christ is to you—your light. Then enter in with holy boldness and walk in Everlasting Light.

O bright and shining light, perfect image of the Father, drive away the blackness of sin from our lives and draw us to You, the light of life. Amen.

THE ANGEL OF HIS PRESENCE

In all their affliction he was afflicted, and the angel of his presence saved them: in his love and in his pity he redeemed them; and he bare them and carried them all the days of old. *(Isaiah 63:9)*

A nervous, restless boy, in his early childhood, called out in the night, "Daddy, are you there?" The father answered, "Yes, I am here. Do you want anything?" "No, I only wanted to be sure you were there." And the frightened boy, still in the dark, went directly to sleep. Oh, child of God, beset by fears and troubled so that you have found no rest, let "The Angel of His Presence" comfort you. Unstop your ears. Speak to Him, and you shall hear the voice of Him who spoke as never man spoke, saying "Lo, I am with you."

May the warmth and joy of Your Presence transform our lives and bring us comfort, security, and peace so that we may walk in Your ways. Amen.

OUR POTTER

But now, O Lord, thou art our father; we are the clay and thou our potter; and we all are the work of thy hand. *(Isaiah 64:8)*

Have you understood the meaning of the force that presses in upon your life today? Has it seemed only pain, only wrong and deep injustice? Behind all that seems to be wrong, "the Potter" stands, with an ideal so lofty that our highest imagination has not fully grasped it. A beautiful, transformed life, one fit to sit with Him upon His throne, is in the Potter's mind, and He is shaping you through trying and difficult experiences. Shall we not learn to say today,

"I am the clay, and You the Potter. Shape me as You will, dear Lord. Shape me in the image of Christ that He may be formed in me, as is Your will. You are the Master Craftsman." Amen.

BALM OF GILEAD

Is there no balm in Gilead? *(Jeremiah 8:22)*

There are experiences of suffering through which the Master wills that we should pass. There are burdens which He does not lift, though He takes us, burden and all, into His everlasting arms. But in every suffering which He permits, He is our "Balm." He eases every pain. He comforts every sorrow. He strengthens us in every weakness. There is a "Balm" in our Gilead. Shall we take from Him the comfort that He offers us today?

O Great Physician, You heal our brokenness and restore wholeness and holiness in body, soul and spirit. Melt away the pain and hurts we undergo as a part of our sinfulness, through Christ our Lord. Amen.

THE PORTION OF JACOB

> The portion of Jacob is not like them: for he is the former of all things; and Israel is the rod of his inheritance; the Lord of hosts is his name. *(Jeremiah 10:16)*

When we are able to lay hold of the fact that Jesus is "our Portion" then do we truly possess all things, for "how shall He not with Him freely give us all things?" Nay, more, "For all things are yours. And you are Christ's and Christ is God's." Shall we seek to appropriate all of His matchless love and grace and hope and courage and joy and fruit and power? What more can we ask or have?

Certainly, Lord, You have given us all things, now and in the future. Let us seek from You those things of eternal value for our inheritance in heaven. Amen.

THE HOPE OF ISRAEL

> O the hope of Israel, the saviour thereof in time of trouble, why shouldst thou be as a stranger in the land, and as a wayfaring man that turneth aside to tarry for a night? *(Jeremiah 14:8)*

"The hope of His people," Israel, is also the Hope of His bride, the church. Jesus Christ has broken down the dividing wall between Jew and Gentile and become the Saviour of all tribes, races, and nations of the earth. And when He shall come He shall be both "Hope" and full completion to every believing soul. Even so come, Lord Jesus, come quickly.

Jesus Christ, with the eyes of faith may we see the substance of things hoped for. Thank You that we are Your chosen people in whom all the promises of God are fulfilled. Amen.

A RIGHTEOUS BRANCH

> Behold, the days come, saith the Lord, that I will raise unto
> David a righteous Branch, and a King shall reign and prosper,
> and shall execute judgment and justice in the earth.
> *(Jeremiah 23:5)*

A "righteous servant" is one who serves righteously, satisfying every command of his master. A "righteous branch" is
one which rightly respects, honors, and bears fruit to the tree
from which it grows. "You are branches," our Saviour said of
us, but He also said, "My Father prunes." He who is the
"Righteous Branch" heard the Father say, "This is my beloved
Son in whom I am well pleased." Shall we not seek with all
our hearts to so abide in Him that we shall glorify the Father
by bearing much fruit?

*Lord God, may we too become righteous branches as we
abide in the true vine who imparts holiness to us. Thus, we
will be justified as You execute judgment. Amen.*

RESTINGPLACE

> My people hath been lost sheep: their shepherds have caused
> them to go astray, they have turned them away on the
> mountains: they have gone from mountain to hill, they have
> forgotten their restingplace. *(Jeremiah 50:6)*

Truly there is rest for the weary, for Jesus is our "Resting
Place." Therefore, in the midst of the toil and the weariness,
in the midst of the struggle and strife, let us ask that our ears
may be opened to hear Him who said, "Come unto me all ye
that labour and are heavy laden, and I will give you rest." To
abide in Him in continuous love and obedient faith is to find
Him our "Resting Place."

*Lord Jesus, we are weary and under stress from the cares
and anxieties of this world. You alone give the peace and
rest we need to grow and prosper spiritually. Revive and refresh us today. Amen.*

A PLANT OF RENOWN

And I will raise up for them a plant of renown, and they shall be no more consumed with hunger in the land, neither bear the shame of the heathen any more. *(Ezekiel 34:29)*

Although our Lord came as a tender plant, and with no form nor comeliness, yet He has become a "Plant of Renown," for already no other name is so widely known, no other name carries such wondrous power, no other name shows such boundless grace, and sometime, perhaps soon, "every knee shall bow and every tongue proclaim" that "the Tender Plant" is a "Plant of Renown," that "Jesus Christ is Lord to the glory of God the Father."

O great gardener, plant Your precious seed of life within me, that it may bear fruit to eternal life. May our harvest be rich and bountiful. Amen.

A STONE CUT WITHOUT HANDS

Thou sawest till that a stone was cut out without hands, which smote the image upon his feet that were of iron and clay, and brake them to pieces . . . and the stone that smote the image became a great mountain, and filled the whole earth. *(Daniel 2:34, 35)*

Men plan for peace in human governments, build courts of arbitration, conferences of nations, pacts and pledges, only to find them crumbling in utter failure before the human work is half complete. The Eternal God is planning a kingdom and government that cannot fail, and He is the King, whose shape and form and size and power are ordered by the Most High God. He will strike in His coming every man-made plan. Are we looking for that "Stone" to come and strike? Shall we be "ready in the day of His power"?

Master stone mason, cut away all that is not pleasing and build us into living temples with Your power providing our foundation. Amen.

ANCIENT OF DAYS

> I saw in the night visions, and, behold, one like the Son of man came with the clouds of heaven, and came to the ancient of days. . . . His dominion is an everlasting dominion, which shall not pass away, and his kingdom that which shall not be destroyed. *(Daniel 7:13, 14)*

"In the beginning was the Word," and He who redeemed us is "The Ancient of Days," whose head is "white as snow" (Revelation 1:14). He was from everlasting and will be unto the ages of ages our eternal God. We, whose life upon the earth is but a hand-breadth, shall bow in worship and adoration at the feet of "The Ancient of Days."

You who existed from the beginning, thank You for choosing us from before the dawn of time. Complete the work You have begun. Help us to obey to this end. Amen.

THE PRINCE OF PRINCES

> He shall also stand up against the Prince of princes; but he shall be broken without hand. *(Daniel 8:25)*

Almighty God has sought to exalt His Son, so that in all things He might rule in our lives, as King of kings, as Lord of lords, and as in this text, "The Prince of princes." In earthly kingdoms it is very often true that upon the prince who is heir apparent to the throne is lavished more affection than upon the king himself. What about our love and affection to "the Prince of princes"? Although sitting now at the right hand of the Father and one with Him, He is waiting to be crowned on earth. Do we pay Him more devotion and deeper love than we do to these erring mortals who reign over us? Let us, in the real things of daily life, exalt Him to His rightful place and pour out our devotion to Him.

Lord, what earthly prince may be compared to You? May we pay You homage with our material, mental, and spiritual gifts. Amen.

THE HOPE OF HIS PEOPLE

The Lord also shall roar out of Zion, and utter his voice from Jerusalem; and the heavens and the earth shall shake: but the Lord will be the hope of his people, and the strength of the children of Israel. *(Joel 3:16)*

There is no hope apart from Him; no hope in self to win against the world, the flesh, and the devil! No hope in self to be or do that which shall bless the world; but there is glorious hope for those who trust in Him. Jesus, our Saviour, King, and Bridegroom, the Living Head of the body of which we are but humble members, is "The Hope of His People."

Our Saviour, You are the hope of glory, the anchor of our souls. We will trust in You alone for all we need pertaining to life and godliness. Amen.

A refuge for his people - NIV

A RULER

But thou, Bethlehem Ephratah, though thou be little among the thousands of Judah, yet out of thee shall he come forth unto me that is to be ruler in Israel; whose goings forth have been from of old, from everlasting. *(Micah 5:2)*

Never in the history of the world have there been such hopeless failures of human governments as now. Never such high ideals, and never have ideals fallen so flat. Great plans are made and conferences held to promote peace and good government, and like flimsy houses of cards the highest hopes are shattered in ruthless, heartless, brutal war. So it must be until He who has the right to reign shall come and "be Ruler," not in Israel alone, but in all the world. A century ago one who was a chosen spokesman of the Lord said, "Perhaps He would have come sooner if we had, from our hearts, prayed more earnestly, 'Thy Kingdom come.'"

Sovereign Lord, as we plan our lives, may You be ruler and master in all our goals and intentions. Amen.

A STRONG HOLD

> The Lord is good, a strong hold in the day of trouble; and he
> knoweth them that trust in him. *(Nahum 1:7)*

During World War II when the German aircraft bombed London, multitudes of people hid in the subways of London. In the Highlands of Central Africa there is a section known as "The Iron Stone Plateau," where the amount of ore appears to attract lightning, and many people in that area dig cellars into which they go when thunderstorms arise. There are dangerous storms which beset our spiritual life from which there is no safe retreat but Christ. Is He your "Strong Hold"? Have you learned to hide in Him?

Blessed Saviour, thank You for binding the "strong man" (the devil) in our lives. Be our strong tower—victor over our foes. Amen.

A refuge - NIV

A WALL OF FIRE

> For I, saith the Lord, will be unto her a wall of fire round
> about, and will be the glory in the midst of her. *(Zechariah
> 2:5)*

All the defense those who trust in Him need is the person God Himself. He is a wall of fire through which the fiercest foe can never come. The foe of evil thoughts will be burned. The hasty tongue will be consumed. The selfish desire that creeps so insidiously through every other barricade will be consumed by Him who is a "Wall of Fire" when we shall hide in Him.

Lord Jesus, You came to baptize with fire to burn away all evil and impurity in our lives for Your sake. Amen.

KING OVER ALL THE EARTH

> And his feet shall stand in that day upon the Mount of Olives. . . . And the Lord shall be king over all the earth: in that day shall there be one Lord, and his name one. *(Zechariah 14:4–9)*

Some day, God grant it may be soon, "His feet shall stand upon the Mount of Olives" and *all the earth* shall know that He is King. Can any flight of swift imagination exceed that picture? Through all the strife of nations, all the pride and rivalry of kings, what peace, what glory, what undreamed of wonders shall be seen when He, "the King of kings," shall reign "over all the earth." Does that day not draw you mightily? Does not the Spirit-given cry fill all your soul—"Even so, come, Lord Jesus!"

Even today Lord, we know You rule over the whole earth. Rule in the deepest places of our hearts for Your glory. Amen.

THE KING

> And it shall come to pass, that every one that is left of all the nations which came against Jerusalem shall even go up from year to year to worship the King, the Lord of hosts, and to keep the feast of tabernacles. *(Zechariah 14:16)*

He is King. It matters not that earth refused to crown Him and to acknowledge His right to reign. He only awaits the Father's day and hour to receive the kingdom which is His. The world waits and weeps, the whole creation groans in pain for lack of the conditions that shall be when men have crowned Him King. We join that grief, but have we truly crowned Him in our lives? Does He reign supremely every day, in every act, and over all our words and thoughts? There will be joy in His heart, joy in heaven, and joy in your heart, when you shall fully and with no reserve crown Jesus King and Lord of All.

O King of all that is, restore Your dominion in our hearts, today and forever. Amen.

THE MESSENGER OF THE COVENANT

> Behold, I will send my messenger, . . . even the messenger of the covenant, whom ye delight in: behold he shall come, saith the Lord of hosts. *(Malachi 3:1)*

He who is our example that we should walk in His steps has called Himself "The Messenger of the Covenant." The Father gave a promise to those who should believe in His Son. The Son came bringing that promise, that covenant—a Messenger sent from heaven. To the true believer that most precious covenant is, "I will write my laws upon their hearts, and upon their minds will I engrave them." Will you accept it now? "Open your mouth wide and I will fill it."

Lord, give us the wisdom and grace to know Your laws, written on our hearts, and to keep them. Amen.

REFINER

> And he shall sit as a refiner and purifier of silver: and he shall purify the sons of Levi, and purge them as gold and silver, that they may offer unto the Lord an offering in righteousness. *(Malachi 3:3)*

When grosser things which men can see are removed from our lives, there is grave danger that we shall be satisfied and forget that still as heaven is high above the earth, so high are His ways above our ways, and His thoughts above our thoughts. That there is a finer life, a deeper, holier peace, a clearer, surer likeness of the Lord possible for His children, needs to be clearly understood. And though through all of life we may seem to have been in the melting pot, shall we not say to Him again at any cost,

"Dear Refiner, make we what You will. Refine me by any process that seems good unto You." Amen.

PURIFIER

And He shall sit as a . . . purifier of silver. (Malachi 3:3)

No work of God shows more plainly His boundless love than His desire to purify our lives. So much dross is found in us that we have need to be tried in the furnace of affliction and to be purged as gold and silver. The difficult experiences through which we pass may often be understood as the infinite love of the Father seeking to separate the dross from our lives, to bring us to a point of purity where we may see and reflect His image.

Purify us, O Lord, that we may become as pure silver. Amen.

THE SUN OF RIGHTEOUSNESS

But unto you that fear my name shall the Sun of righteousness arise with healing in his wings. (Malachi 4:2)

Jesus said that when the Holy Spirit ("the Comforter") has come "He will reprove the world . . . of righteousness, because I go to my Father." Among all the sons of men "there is none righteous, no not one." But He who performed the creation of the worlds, and walked the streets of Judea, sits at the "right hand of the Father" in His glory. He is the Sun whose radiant righteousness heals our sin-sick souls.

Lord Jesus, we come with our earth stains and our innumerable faults and infirmities and bow at Your feet and worship You while we seek the "healing in Your wings." Amen.

THE SON OF DAVID

> The book of the generation of Jesus Christ, the son of David.
> *(Matthew 1:1)*

Our Lord was a lineal descendant of David the king. This entitled Him to the right of sovereignty over David's land, and when He was here among men, we are told, there was no other claimant to the throne of David. Herod sought to destroy the Child-King, Jesus, but Egypt was chosen as a refuge place for Him. The heart of Herod was like the hearts of all the children of men who will not have Him to rule over them. Christ was bearing us upon His heart, even as a child, for He is the same "yesterday, today and forever," and He is our refuge now.

Jesus Christ, Son of David, may our hearts be linked up with Your great heart always. Amen.

SON OF ABRAHAM

> The book of the generation of Jesus Christ . . . the son of Abraham. *(Matthew 1:1)*

Three titles in one verse, "Jesus Christ—Son of David—Son of Abraham." Abraham was the head of the covenant nation. God had given to him the promise that in his seed should all the nations of the earth be blessed. Jesus submitted to the Jewish law in righteousness. He lived as a Jew, He preached to the Jews. He died for the Jews as well as for all people. "So then they which be of faith are blessed with faithful Abraham" (Galatians 3:9). How wonderful! God manifested in the flesh as Abraham's seed and yet the One who made the promise to Abraham!

O promised Son of Abraham and Son of God, our Saviour, hold us fast in faith in Your Word. Amen.

JESUS

Thou shalt call his name Jesus; for he shall save his people from their sins. *(Matthew 1:21)*

Over seven hundred times in the New Testament is this name used—"Jesus" (Joshua). How familiar we are with that name! Joshua of the Old Testament, who saved Israel by leading them through the River Jordan, fought their battles and was steadfast in his allegiance to God and His people. He was a type of our Lord, who is our Joshua; who fights our battles for us; who is our Leader, our Protector, our Saviour! Who will never cease His lordship until He has us safely in the sheepfold on the other side. Hallelujah! What a Saviour!

This day, You Saviour of our souls, in whom we are separated for eternity, guide us by Your Holy Spirit to the praise of Your grace. Amen.

EMMANUEL

Behold, a virgin . . . shall bring forth a son, and they shall call his name Emmanuel. *(Matthew 1:23)*

This was the prophecy of Isaiah 7:14: "Therefore the Lord himself shall give you a sign; Behold, a virgin shall conceive, and bear a son, and shall call his name Immanuel." "Emmanuel" (God with us)! What a wonderful God and Saviour He is. He is with us as He promised in Matthew 28:19–20: "Go ye, therefore, and teach all nations, baptizing them in the name of the Father, and of the Son, and of the Holy Ghost: Teaching them to observe all things whatsoever I have commanded you: and, lo, I am with you alway, even unto the end of the world." Let us sense His presence and make Him real. Walk, talk, live with and love Him more and more as the days go by.

Lord Jesus, we know that You dwell in us. May we enjoy Your fellowship today. Amen.

A GOVERNOR

> And thou, Bethlehem . . . out of thee shall come a Governor, that shall rule my people Israel. *(Matthew 2:6)*

Bethlehem of Judah! A little village, twice highly honored! The birthplace of David, king of Israel, and the birthplace of Jesus the Christ, King of kings and Lord of lords! Who could visit this Land of Promise and not desire to see this city of cities, the place where Jehovah enthroned in human form and lying in a manger gazed into the face of the virgin Mary, His mother. The government shall be upon His shoulders and He will reign in righteousness. Blessed day!

We pray for its soon coming and ask for grace that we may hasten it. Amen.

A ruler - NIV

THE YOUNG CHILD

> When they had heard the king, they departed; and, lo, the star which they saw in the east, went before them, till it came and stood over where the young child was. *(Matthew 2:9)*

A star in the east led the wise men to a Star that shall outshine all the stars of Heaven. Look at this Young Child! Hold fast your attention as you gaze upon His face, lying there, His eyes looking into your own inquiring eyes. Visualize, if you can, God manifested in the flesh before you. God—the Young Child! The Creator of all things! Before whom are thirty years of human life in which He will work with His fellow men. Mystery of mysteries!

O wonderful One, as we bow before You today, help us to discern something of Your devotion for the sons of men. Amen.

A NAZARENE

And he came and dwelt in a city called Nazareth: that it might be fulfilled which was spoken by the prophets, He shall be called a Nazarene. *(Matthew 2:23)*

Nazareth was a town in the northern border of the plain of Esdraelon. Here came the angel Gabriel and announced to Mary the coming birth of Christ: "And the angel came in unto her, and said, Hail, thou that art highly favoured, the Lord is with thee: blessed art thou among women." (Luke 1:28) On the night of His betrayal our Lord asked the question, "Whom do you seek?" They replied, "Jesus of Nazareth" and He said, "I am He."

Jesus of Nazareth, may we never be ashamed to be called the followers of the lowly Nazarene. We too are "highly favored" to be your followers. Help us to live up to our calling. Amen.

FRIEND OF SINNERS

Behold . . . a friend of publicans and sinners. *(Matthew 11:19)*

These are the words of Jesus Himself. He quotes their own phrases as applied to Himself. What a title! How wonderfully true it is—"A Friend of sinners!" So He was and so He is—a Friend who sticks closer than a brother. Laying aside the royal robes of heaven, He came here to befriend sinful men. It was a lifework that cost Him His life. Hallelujah! What a Friend! How gladly He paid the price of friendship. As we take up the work of the day, let us ask ourselves the question, "Am I a friend of sinners?" If not, then I am not like my Lord, for He was and He delighted in it.

Lord Jesus, the world is full of friendless sinners. May we make them acquainted with You who are their Friend. May our lives demonstrate Your love. Amen.

GOD'S SERVANT

Behold my servant, whom I have chosen. *(Matthew 12:18)*

Jesus, the prophesied Servant! Isaiah had portrayed Him. Jehovah had chosen Him. All of God's ways were known unto Him from the beginning. You hear the echo of His voice: "I delight to do Your will, O my God!" Nothing was too great for Him to do, for He was the Creator, and nothing was too hard for Him, for He had all power. Nothing was too small for Him to do, for He stooped to notice a widow's mite and give a mighty lesson from it. What a gracious privilege to be yoked with Him in service.

Dear Lord, let us labor with You, the Servant of Jehovah, today and thus make it a good day for You and for us, as You would be pleased with our work. Amen.

GOD'S BELOVED

Behold . . . my beloved, in whom my soul is well pleased. *(Matthew 12:18)*

God's Son was a *beloved* Servant. How dear He was to the Father—dear as the apple of His eye. Yet His love for us was manifest in His surrender to pay the penalty of our sin. "Greater love has no man than this." "While we were yet sinners, Christ died for us." In the hour of darkness He cried, "My God, My God, why have You forsaken Me?" The agony, the grief, the pain He suffered, all had a voice that rings out the message, "God so loved."

Our Father, Your love for us has broken all the barriers down; and we pray that Your Spirit may rest upon us this day as we meditate upon the greatness of Your love. Amen.

The one I love - NIV

68

A SOWER

He that soweth the good seed is the Son of man. *(Matthew 13:37)*

The seed is the Word of God. God's Son sowed the good seed. He sows the Word of Truth in the hearts of men. When we sow the gospel we sow good seed. Nothing is comparable to the *Word* itself. It has potential power. It is a *living* seed and never fails. We are to imitate our Lord, the Sower, and see that the pure seed of the Word is scattered wherever we go. "Sow beside all waters."

Lord, make me a seed-sower this day, and hear my prayer for all the sowers in all the world! Amen.

THE SON OF THE LIVING GOD

Thou art the Christ, the Son of the living God. *(Matthew 16:16)*

This is the title of the long-looked for Saviour—the Anointed One. Prophets had foretold His coming, and now His kingly authority is recorded. Over three hundred times is this title used in the New Testament. From "Christ" comes the word "Christian," and from "Christian" comes the word "Christianity." Today this land of ours is the foremost Christian nation of the world. Our gospel is the Gospel of Christ of which we are not ashamed, for it is the power of God unto salvation to everyone that believes.

Lord, as "Christ-ones" let us honor You by having the same anointing power resting upon us as we enter the service of the day. Amen.

JESUS THE CHRIST

> Then charged he his disciples that they should tell no man
> that he was Jesus the Christ. *(Matthew 16:20)*

This title, "Jesus the Christ," is used a hundred times in the
New Testament. "The Saviour—the Anointed One"—a com-
bination that magnifies the office of the One whom we long
to worship. The time had not yet come for them to preach the
story of redemption. They were to hold their peace for a season, but He tells *us* to go into all the world and tell to all people the wonderful message of Jesus Christ and His finished
work. Are we obeying the command?

*Dear Father, as we go forth today with this precious Name
in our hearts and on our lips, help us to tell someone of the
wonders of the Man, Your Son, Jesus the Christ! Amen.*

GOD'S BELOVED SON

> This is my beloved Son, in whom I am well pleased; hear ye
> him. *(Matthew 17:5)*

Wonderful manifestation! A cloud of glory overshadowing
that which was too deep for human eyes to penetrate. The
voice of Jehovah attesting that Jesus was His beloved Son
and that His words were to be heard. The same voice and the
same message were heard in Matthew 3:17 when our Lord
was baptized, and once again in John 12:28 in the Garden.
"His beloved" and *our* beloved! How marvelous is that testimony to Him whom we have learned to love, and because we
love Him, we are beloved of the Father.

*Lord, may we breathe it over and over again today, "I am
my beloved's and my beloved is mine." Amen.*

THE PROPHET OF NAZARETH

This is Jesus the prophet of Nazareth of Galilee. *(Matthew 21:11)*

This great demonstration had been planned by God and foretold by Him (Zechariah 9:9). Our Lord comes into Jerusalem riding upon the foal of a donkey. The crowd is vast; the enthusiasm is great. "Who is this?" is the cry; and the answer is, "This is Jesus, the Prophet of Nazareth." A despised Nazarene! A prophet from an obscure village! We are all proud if, by chance, we were born in some noted place; but God, when He took the form of a man, was born in a manger and made His home in Nazareth. For our sakes He became poor, that through His poverty, we might be made rich.

Let us meditate upon the riches of His grace, bow at His feet and kiss them as we adore Him; and may we walk humbly this day with the despised Nazarene. Amen.

THE BRIDEGROOM

And while they went to buy, the bridegroom came. *(Matthew 25:10)*

The Bridegroom must come. The true church is Christ's beloved espoused bride. He has waited a long, long time for her to prepare herself for the glad day and to add the last one who will complete the body. Are you thinking of Him today as the Coming One? And of yourself as one of those who are to be blessed as His beloved throughout eternity? How insignificant are all the little cares and trials! How small they seem when our eyes are turned with expectancy toward Him as He comes in the clouds. "Blessed are they which are called unto the marriage supper of the Lamb" (Revelation 19:9). Hallelujah!

May our prayer always be, "Even so, come, Lord Jesus, come quickly." Amen.

THE HOLY ONE OF GOD

I know thee who thou art, the Holy One of God. *(Mark 1:24)*

What a testimony coming from the lips of one possessed of an unclean spirit, Satan's tool, under his power. But the presence of Christ overawed him. "I know You who You are, the Holy One of God." This was not a willing testimony, but it was forced from him. Many men are devil-possessed, and the devil has powers accorded him, but Christ can hinder his followers, can cast out his demons and forbid their speaking (v. 34). How lovingly we should bow at the feet of the Holy One of God! May we fix our thoughts upon Him and say many times today as we walk and talk with Him,

"O Holy One of God, glorify Yourself through us and cleanse any impurities from us that we too may be made holy." Amen.

OUR BROTHER

For whosoever shall do the will of God, the same is my brother. *(Mark 3:35)*

If this is true, and it is, then the reverse is also true, and He is our Brother. The picture is given in the thirty-first and thirty-fourth verse: "There came then his brethren and his mother, and, standing without, sent unto him, calling him . . . And he looked round about on them which sat about him, and said, Behold my mother and my brethren." How wonderful that He should graciously give this title to those who do the Father's will! And what is that will? The acceptance of His Son as our Saviour and Lord, and the submission of our will to His will as revealed in His Word, for His Word is His will. How near and dear He is to us, our Lord and our Brother! Hold it fast in your meditation—"Ours by faith; ours forever."

Dear Lord, keep us in loving fellowship with You this day. Amen.

SON OF THE MOST HIGH GOD

> And cried with a loud voice, and said, What have I do to with thee, Jesus, thou Son of the most high God? *(Mark 5:7)*

Here we are confronted with another testimony from an unclean spirit—"Son of the most high God," he calls Jesus. What unseen powers compelled this significant title? Was it brought about by being face to face with Him? Judas betrayed Him, but this poor, demon-possessed man worshiped Him. In these strange days many teachers, professors, and preachers refuse to honor Him as *the Son,* but only as *a Son* of God. But we lift our hearts to Him and say,

"Son of the most high God, be our companion this day. May we withhold nothing from You." Amen.

THE CARPENTER

> Is not this the carpenter? *(Mark 6:3)*

The Carpenter! Two things are suggested in this verse. Joseph is not mentioned and is probably not now living. Jesus worked at the carpenter's bench and continued to do so until He assumed His place in His public ministry. We can and should visualize Him in His daily tasks—a man among men. How near He seems to us! What a joy to know that He handled the hammer and sharpened the saw, planed the plank and helped to supply the food for the family. Test this picture of Him with any false system and observe the contrast. No matter what our calling may be, the Carpenter will be one with us. We can walk arm in arm with Him to the daily task.

O Carpenter of Galilee, You are our ideal always! Amen.

THE SON OF MARY

Is not this the carpenter, the son of Mary? *(Mark 6:3)*

The Carpenter, the "Son of Mary," had come back to His home town from an evangelistic trip in which He had worked many miracles. The people were astonished at His teaching. Prejudice possessed them. "Is not this the Son of Mary?" We never worship Mary as do our Catholic friends, but we do honor her above all women—God's chosen vessel to bring forth His Son and fulfill His prophecy. How true He was to the last. See Him on the cross and hear His last words to Mary, "Woman, behold your son" (John the beloved, to whom He had said, "Behold your mother").

Blessed title—Son of Mary! Christ, we worship You as the Babe who is one day to rule the world and at whose feet we shall bow in worshipful adoration! Amen.

GOOD MASTER

Good Master, what shall I do that I may inherit eternal life? *(Mark 10:17)*

This question was asked of our Lord by a young man with great possessions, as recorded in Matthew 19:17. This is the concrete question of the soul of man, "What shall I do to secure a right to heaven?" The theme of *religion* is *do;* but the theme of our Lord was just the opposite: "Follow Me." Eternal life is a gift. Those who accept and follow Him find that He *is* the "Good Master" because He provided for us a salvation— simple to accept but costing Him a price which involved His own life. How gracious is our God, and how we should love and adore Him!

Lord, may we walk in the sunshine of Your love today. Amen.

THE SON OF MAN

> The Son of man shall be delivered unto the chief priests, and unto the scribes; and they shall condemn him to death.
> *(Mark 10:33)*

In the ninth chapter Jesus had said, "The Son of man is delivered into the hands of men, and they shall kill him." How earnestly He sought to stress the fact of His approaching sacrifice upon His disciples, and how He longed for their sympathy; but, alas, alas, how hard is the human heart! How difficult it is for Him to win us to Himself! "The Son of man must suffer many things," He had said, but the saddest of all was the failure of His own beloved disciples to enter into the burden He bore as He approached the cross.

O Holy Son of man, give unto us the loving hearts that will enter into fellowship with You in all things. Amen.

A RANSOM

> The Son of man came . . . to give his life a ransom for many.
> *(Mark 10:45)*

"A ransom for many!" Here Christ is set forth as the penalty paid for the sins of the world. He saw that we were sinners under the judgment wrath of God, and He took our place and paid the penalty and price for our deliverance with His own blood. Listen to the drops of blood as they fall from hands and feet and wounded side! They voice the words, "The ransom price for *my* sins and for the sins of the whole world." We wish that men everywhere would believe it and receive it. How dear, how precious is He to us, washed clean in His blood and freed forever from the punishment due us.

Lord, may our ransomed souls well up in praise to Your glorious Name! Amen.

ONE SON, HIS WELLBELOVED

Having yet therefore one son, his wellbeloved, he sent him also last unto them, saying, They will reverence my son. *(Mark 12:6)*

The Saviour is in Jerusalem. The chief priests and scribes come to Him and question His authority. Jesus answers them in the parable of the vineyard, picturing the treatment of the servants who were sent to gather the fruit, telling the story—so old, so sad—of the attitude of the human heart toward God. He sent His Son, His well-beloved Son, and they took Him and killed Him and cast Him out. How could they? They have cast Him out of the schools and many of the churches, though all we have of earthly civilization and comforts today we owe to Him.

God's well-beloved Son, we enthrone You today in our hearts. Help us to worship and adore You. May we also greatly experience Your love for us. Amen.

A son, whom he loved - NIV

CHRIST, THE SON OF THE BLESSED

Art thou the Christ, the Son of the Blessed? *(Mark 14:61)*

The court is convened. The high priest presides. Charges had been brought against the Lord Jesus Christ by false witnesses but they had not agreed. The high priest put to Him a question, "Are You the Christ, the Son of the Blessed?" And He answered, "I am." He did not deny the title but made a straight confession of His sonship, heirship, power, and coming glory. And when He comes we may be among those who will be caught up in the clouds to meet Him in the air, and with the hosts of Heaven acclaim Him "Blessed!"

Lord, Jesus Christ, You Son of the Blessed, hasten the glad day and grant us Your precious blessings through the blood covenant of our Lord Jesus. Amen.

The Christ, the Son of the Blessed One - NIV

THE KING OF THE JEWS

> And Pilate asked him, Art thou the King of the Jews? And he answering said unto them, Thou sayest it. *(Mark 15:2)*

What a title for our Lord to put His seal upon at the time when the Jews were in subjection to the Romans and He Himself was a prisoner before a judge. But He *is* "King of the Jews"—yes, *King of kings and Lord of all.* Pilate will yet stand before Him to be judged, and the Jewish people will yet proclaim Him as their own King. He is the Ruler. Let us give Him His rightful place as Ruler in our lives. How can we serve Him today? Perhaps in some definite prayer for the Jewish people and some testimony to them of the joy there is in knowing, loving, and serving Him.

Lord, remember Your ancient people and all who seek to make You known to them. Help us to clearly testify who You are. Amen.

THE SON OF THE HIGHEST

> He shall be great, and shall be called the Son of the Highest. *(Luke 1:32)*

In this message of the angel to Mary we see a remarkable co-incidence. In Mark 5:7, the evil spirit in the man in the tombs gives a similar title to Jesus, "Son of the Most High God." The title here given Him is in fulfillment of Psalm 132:11: "The Lord has sworn in truth unto David; he will not turn from it; of the fruit of your body will I set upon your throne." David's heir is to reign as Son of the Most High God, and that time only waits for the completion of the church which is His body. Let us do our best each day to win souls for Him and thus hasten the day when we shall be with Him and reign with Him.

Son of the Highest, we bow to You, we worship You. Help us to magnify Your name today. Amen.

The Son of the Most High - NIV

GOD MY SAVIOUR

And my spirit hath rejoiced in God my Saviour. *(Luke 1:47)*

The word "Saviour" here is "Soter" meaning "presence." Should we not imitate Mary, the blessed woman, in magnifying our Saviour and rejoicing in the finished work which He has accomplished on our behalf? It is never what *we* are but what *He* is. Our joy is in Him, and we rejoice with joy unspeakable and full of glory as we face this day with joyful hearts. Shall we not have a tender heart for those who do not know Him?

Saviour, like a shepherd lead us today to glorify Your name in our efforts to win souls for You. Amen.

HORN OF SALVATION

And hath raised up an horn of salvation for us in the house of his servant David. *(Luke 1:69)*

Here is a title which suggests the strength and power of our Lord—"Horn of Salvation." The word "horn" as used in the Scripture signifies "strength" and is often found in Hebrew literature. In the horns, the bull manifests his strength. The Lord Jesus Christ is our strength and a very present help in time of trouble (Psalm 28:7; 37:39; 92:10; 118:14). "But the salvation of the righteous is of the Lord; He is their strength in the time of trouble." You may be tempted and tried today. You may have burdens to bear. Let Him be your "horn of salvation."

Lord, strengthen us by the power of Your might for today's service for You. May the horn of Your salvation resound through the whole earth. Amen.

THE PROPHET OF THE HIGHEST

> And thou, child, shalt be called the prophet of the Highest.
> *(Luke 1:76)*

Listen to the voice of Zacharias, father of John the Baptist, as he voices the wonderful prophecy concerning his son who was to be the prophet of the Lord to prepare the way before Him. Our Lord is here named "the Highest," or, better, "the Most High." He came from the heights of glory to be born in a manger. "Prophet" in the New Testament means "a public expounder" and to us, His redeemed ones, has been committed this honorable title. We are the expounders of this great revelation of the Bible concerning our most highly exalted Lord.

Glory to God in the Highest, King of kings and Lord of lords, whom we claim as our own. Amen.

A prophet of the Most High - NIV

THE DAYSPRING FROM ON HIGH

> Through the tender mercy of our God; whereby the dayspring from on high hath visited us. *(Luke 1:78)*

Zacharias is inspired as his soul goes forth to speak of the coming of the Messiah. It has been suggested that the glory of the sunrise was breaking over the hills surrounding Jerusalem and the golden glory lighted up the horizon as his lips breathed the words inspired by the Spirit of God, "Dayspring from on high!" Perhaps the morning glory brought to the mind of Zacharias the message of Isaiah, "Arise, shine, for your light is come and the glory of the Lord is risen upon you."

Father, before we take up our daily tasks, we turn our eyes to the heavens with grateful hearts and let the Holy Spirit flood our souls with the glory of the risen, coming Christ. Amen.

Rising sun . . . from heaven - NIV

CHRIST THE LORD

For unto you is born this day in the city of David a Saviour, which is Christ the Lord. *(Luke 2:11)*

The heavens are opened now and the message of the angel of the Lord is announced—"good tidings of great joy." The message was to the humble shepherds, and it will mean much to us if we can, in humility of heart, take our place with the shepherds, acknowledge our unworthiness, and appropriate the truth to our own souls—"Unto you is born a Saviour, Christ the Lord" (the Anointed One—the Ruler). We are no longer to rule ourselves. He is to rule us.

Lord, with joy we submit our wills and surrender all to You. Help us to magnify You this day. Amen.

THE BABE

Ye shall find the babe wrapped in swaddling clothes, lying in a manger. *(Luke 2:12)*

Again the voice of the angel rings out to the shepherds; "Christ the Lord—the Babe—lying in a manger." How easy it would be for the shepherds to find Him. No other newly born baby would be found "lying in a manger"—just One—and He, the altogether lovely One, the chiefest among ten thousand! Sometimes the saints magnify their human birthright and place of birth, but He was to be a blessing to the humblest. Would not the cattle—could they have sensed the significance of the event—have bent their knees in homage to the Babe? How sad to know that millions in our own land have not yet bowed the knee to Him.

Lord, may we who have named Your name bow in humblest submission to You today and pour out our hearts in joyful praise to You, the Babe of Bethlehem. Amen.

A baby - NIV

80

THE CONSOLATION OF ISRAEL

> There was a man in Jerusalem, whose name was Simeon; and the same man was just and devout, waiting for the consolation of Israel. *(Luke 2:25)*

Simeon was just and devout and waited for the "Consolation of Israel." "Consolation" means "paraclete" (one coming alongside) and is a term we usually use to think and speak of the Holy Spirit who comes to abide in and lead us out in our daily life. Simeon was waiting for the deliverance of the Jews by the coming of the Messiah. They did not as a nation receive Him, but some did and were consoled. Israel shall yet have the promised consolation, as Paul was comforted by the power of the indwelling Holy Spirit sent from Christ (1 Thessalonians 1:5).

Lord, may we also rely upon the abiding comfort of Christ all the day. Amen.

THE SALVATION OF GOD

> For mine eyes have seen thy salvation. *(Luke 2:30)*

The aged saint Simeon, standing in the temple, took the child Jesus in his arms and, looking into His face, lifted his eyes to heaven and said: "Lord, now let your servant depart in peace, according to your word; for *mine eyes have seen your salvation.*" Long had he waited, long had he prayed, long had he desired to see Him. Now the Spirit of God revealed to him the fact that his heart's desire had been granted and that he was gazing upon the Divine Saviour of souls and that death had no more terrors for him. There is but one cure for the world's unrest, "The Salvation of God." The poor, hungry-hearted, sin-sick souls are waiting.

Lord, guide us in this service to Your glory. May You come alongside to bring consolation in our defeats and encouragement in our victories. Amen.

A LIGHT TO LIGHTEN THE GENTILES

> A light to lighten the Gentiles, and the glory of thy people Israel. *(Luke 2:32)*

The world has been a dark world ever since Adam and Eve listened to the temptation of Satan. There was no hope until God said: "The seed of the woman shall bruise the serpent's head"—a promise of coming victory for a lost race. He who is the light of the Gentiles is the light of the world (Matthew 4:16). The light shone for Israel first, but Israel rejected its blessed beams. But again the Light shall shine for the people now wandering over the earth in darkness. What is the duty of believers? Is it not to lift the Light high so that the world of sinners in darkness may come into fellowship with Him?

Lord of Light, help us to shine as lights in a dark world this day until the brightness of Your coming. Amen.

A light for revelation to the Gentiles - NIV

THE GLORY OF GOD'S PEOPLE ISRAEL

> A light to lighten the Gentiles, and the glory of thy people Israel. *(Luke 2:32)*

The message of Paul was "to the Jew first," but here the Gentiles are mentioned first. The Jews turned away from Jesus and would not have Him to rule over them, but the Gentiles will not receive Him either—just a few. The glory shall rest upon Israel when He comes with scepter in hand to rule a reconstructed earth. The Shekinah glory, manifested in the tabernacle and temple, will shine again upon His beloved people and Jesus—the Jew—will be the glory of Israel in that day. Let us love the Jews and seek to bring the gospel of the grace of God to them.

Lord Jesus, who are the Glory of Your people Israel, remember Your persecuted people and help us to love them. Help us to bring the gospel to the whole world. Amen.

A SIGN

This child is set . . . for a sign which shall be spoken against. *(Luke 2:34)*

Our Lord Jesus Christ was a clear sign to Israel. The prophecies had long before made evident that Israel was to be tested when the Messiah came. Some would believe and follow Him. Some would reject and crucify Him. When Pilate asked our Lord, "Are You a King?" His answer was: "To this end was I born, and for this cause came I into the world." Poor Pilate, he had his evidence but would not accept it. Where is he? The Sign has been given to our land, also. Where are the multitudes? The same old story will be told again and again, but many will not accept it.

O Lord, have compassion upon this poor land. Inspire Your servants to be brave and true in sounding the alarm. By Your grace call many to Your kingdom. Amen.

THE CHILD JESUS

The child Jesus tarried behind in Jerusalem. *(Luke 2:43)*

Here we have our first view of Jesus as a young lad, interested in the business of His Heavenly Father. Hear Him when Joseph and Mary seek Him: "Know you not that I must be about my Father's business?" The story of His life is a constant surprise. God manifested in the flesh—a Child; with words of wisdom falling from His lips—a message for us all: "Occupy (do business) till I come." Every disciple is a businessman or woman, and our business is the most important in all the world. Let us take as a motto for our daily life the words of the Child Jesus, "I must be about my Father's business."

Lord, help us to be busy about Your business this day and to do the business of the kingdom in the marketplace and everywhere You open doors. Amen.

The boy Jesus - NIV

PHYSICIAN

And he said unto them, Ye will surely say unto me this
proverb, Physician, heal thyself. *(Luke 4:23)*

Our Lord had been in Galilee. His fame had spread throughout that region. He had done mighty miracles. He came back
home to Nazareth, where He had been brought up, and
preached in the synagogue on the Sabbath Day from Isaiah
61:1–3, saying, "This day is this Scripture fulfilled in your
ears." The people who heard these words said, "Is this not
Joseph's son?" Jesus quoted to them our verse, a proverb
among the Jews. What a mistake they made. He *was* the
Great Physician. He *is* the "Great Physician"—"Able to do exceeding abundantly above all we can ask or think." How few
know Him as such a One! How few look to Him!

*Lord, You who are the Great Physician; we look to You to-
day to supply our every need. Amen.*

LORD OF THE SABBATH

And He said unto them, That the Son of man is Lord also of
the Sabbath. *(Luke 6:5)*

He is the "Master (Lord) of the Sabbath." He is the Maker of
heaven and earth. "Without Him nothing was made that is
made." He is either what He claimed to be, or else He is the
greatest imposter who ever lived. It is lawful to do good on
the Sabbath. Serving others is serving the Lord of the Sabbath.
He, with His disciples, plucked and ate wheat on the Sabbath; and on the Sabbath He healed the man with the with-
ered hand. The Sabbath is the Lord's Day. Solve all your
problems in connection with the Lord's Day by the question,
"What would the Lord do on this day?" Then whatever you
do, whether you eat or drink, do all to the glory of God.

*Lord Jesus, we pray that every day may be a good day for
You through our lives. Amen.*

A GREAT PROPHET

> And they glorified God, saying, That a great prophet is risen up among us; and, That God hath visited his people. *(Luke 7:16)*

Four centuries had elapsed since Malachi had passed away, and Israel had been without a prophetic voice. Now they are stirred by the presence of Jesus and glorify God. Israel was not forsaken. God's Word was true. And Jesus was a great Prophet; yes, greater even than they knew. Humble, quiet, gentle, no pomp, no display, but wonderful in works. Do *we* recognize His greatness? Do we believe His prophecies and promises? Do we possess them and profit by them and give glory to His name?

Lord, help us to believe every word of the Prophetic Book and put Your commands into practice. Amen.

THE CHRIST OF GOD

> He said unto them, But whom say ye that I am? Peter answering said, The Christ of God. *(Luke 9:20)*

Jesus was alone in prayer and asked His disciples the question, "Who do the people say that I am?" And after they had given their answers, He asked the question in our text. The disciples were compelled to recognize His heavenly gifts, His greatness, His power, and His gracious Spirit, but it was hard for them to think of Him as One who must suffer persecution and death at the hands of the Jews. But He knew all that was before Him and walked steadily on toward the cruel cross upon which He must die. Today the *professing* church is inclined to reject the theme of His atoning blood, but those of us to whom He is "the Christ of God" adore Him more and more as the depths of His sacrifice and suffering are revealed.

Lord, may we hold You in our hearts today as "the Christ of God," the one given over for our sins. Amen.

THE MASTER OF THE HOUSE

> When once the master of the house is risen up, . . . he shall answer and say unto you, I know not whence ye are. *(Luke 13:25)*

Here is a new title for our Lord—"Master of the House." How appropriate it is: "Lord of the house—the Head—the Governor." The "house" is heaven where He is to rule. The appeal is for earnest effort upon the part of believers to impress upon the unsaved the fact that there is a heaven and there is a hell, and only *one gate* to heaven—Jesus Christ. Why do we not make more definite to people the awful consequences of failure to hear His voice *now,* and that there will come a time when it will be too late?

Dear Lord, may we labor and pray earnestly today that we may be faithful in urging upon people the necessity of decision for Christ. Amen.

The owner of the house - NIV

A GUEST

> And when they saw it, they all murmured, saying, That he was gone to be guest with a man that is a sinner. *(Luke 19:7)*

Zacchaeus was highly honored when Christ invited Himself to be his Guest. How like our Lord! He knew Zacchaeus wanted to see Him and He sought him out and became his guest. How we would congratulate ourselves were some noted person to come to our house to dine. What a fuss we would make. How we would boast about it. Why do we not tell the story to everybody, "A Great One has come to live in my house"? "Who is He?" "He is the King of glory. He holds the worlds in the hollow of His hand. He lives with me."

O blessed Guest, help us today to magnify and glorify You before all. Sweep our hearts clean to make a home for You. Amen.

A NOBLEMAN

> He said therefore, A certain nobleman went into a far country to receive for himself a kingdom, and to return. *(Luke 19:12)*

The setting of this picture is remarkable. Our Lord is standing with the Jews around Him, in the shadow of a palace built by a nobleman, Archelaus, who had gone to Rome and received the kingdom from Caesar. Our Lord is the Nobleman whose face was turned toward the land beyond the skies where He has gone and from whence He will one day return. "Occupy till I come" is His message. He has entrusted to us, as His servants, the most valuable treasures of heaven—time, opportunity, the gifts of the Holy Spirit, a great wide world in which to transact the greatest of all business! Precious privileges are ours and a solemn accounting must be given.

Lord, give us keenness of vision to see and wisdom to use our opportunities in the investment of our lives for You. Amen.

THE CHOSEN OF GOD

> Let him save himself, if he be Christ, the chosen of God. *(Luke 23:35)*

Christ is on the cross. He prays, "Father, forgive them." The people stand beholding Him, the rulers deride Him and mock Him. What a picture! What an insult! *"If* You are the Christ, the *chosen of God"?* People do likewise today. The question mark grows as the days go by, but the title which was given to Him in derision is a wonderfully true one, and it is found again in 1 Peter 2:4. Yes, indeed! Chosen before the foundation of the earth, and the *only One* who could be chosen for the great work of our redemption.

Lord, You have chosen Him, and You have chosen us. May we adore and glory in You this day. Amen.
The Christ of God, the Chosen One - NIV

A PROPHET MIGHTY IN DEED AND WORD

> And he said unto them, What things? And they said unto him, Concerning Jesus of Nazareth, which was a prophet mighty in deed and word before God and all the people. *(Luke 24:19)*

Some hated Him. Some worshiped Him. Mighty in life, mighty in death and mighty in His resurrection! The rulers thought they had eliminated Him. Some seek to do so today. They crucified Him in fulfillment of Scripture, but He is alive today. He lives in the hearts of millions who would be willing to be crucified for Him. He will live throughout the eternal ages, and every word He ever uttered will be fulfilled to the letter.

O mighty Prophet, help us to lay hold of the Word with intensified faith and hold fast until You shall come. Amen.

A prophet, powerful in word and deed - NIV

THE WORD

> In the beginning was the Word, and the Word was with God, and the Word was God. *(John 1:1)*

We come today to John's gospel in which we shall find many titles for the Son of God. Here we confront the first—"the Word." The book of Genesis commences with creation, but John begins with the Creator. Back of all things with which we ever have had or will have to do is *the Word.* "The Word was God!" What a foundation for our faith when we know that Jesus was the Word and the Word was God. Every day we can, if we will, be facing this tremendous fact, and as we feel the throb of our heart, there is a voice which says, "God!" As we look upon the heavens and the clouds—"God!" The sun, the moon, the trees, the flowers, the living creatures, all are saying, "God!" Without Him—nothing! With Him—all things!

O Living Word, who has given us the written Word, help us to abide in You today. Amen.

THE LIGHT OF MEN

In him was life; and the life was the light of men. (John 1:4)

God said, "Let there be light; and there was light" (Genesis 1:3). All life proceeds from our Lord, and all light, also. The Word is a life- and light-giving Word—"The light of the world is Jesus." Visualize the whole world in the darkness of sin, men groping blindly, restless and hopeless. We have the Light of Life. We see Him face to face. We bask in the sunshine of His glory. Pity the spiritually blind and pray for them. Carry the light of the glorious gospel to their darkened souls. Tell them to arise and shine for the Light is come and the glory of the Lord shall shine upon them.

Help us, Lord, to walk in the light as we have fellowship with You and with one another. Let the scales fall from the eyes of unbelievers. Amen.

THE TRUE LIGHT

That was the true Light, which lighteth every man that cometh into the world. (John 1:9)

"The *true* Light." This is in contrast with *false* lights. How many there are in our day. Satan is busy sending them forth through false cults, false teachers, and false teaching. False lights dazzle the eyes but never reveal truth or bring radiance to the soul. The gloom of sin, the uncertainty of life, the dark outlook for the future, confront the sinner stumbling along, without God and without hope. God has ordained us as lights. Let our lights shine today, and may we help some blinded ones to see Jesus as the true Light of the world.

Lord Jesus, in the light of Your Word, and in the light of Yourself, may we witness for You today. Amen.

THE ONLY BEGOTTEN OF THE FATHER

> And the Word was made flesh, and dwelt among us (and we beheld his glory, the glory as of the only begotten of the Father,) full of grace and truth. *(John 1:14)*

This is the most sublime of all the statements of Scripture—"God became flesh!" John saw His glory. How wonderful! That glory was manifest in the person of the Only Begotten of the Father—Jesus Christ. He is the Unique Figure in the world's history—the sinless, perfect One—perfect God and perfect man. "Great is the mystery of godliness; God was manifest in the flesh." He must be God to forgive sin, and He must be man to atone for sin. So the God-Man is our Saviour.

We worship You, we adore You, the only begotten of the Father. Help us to walk and talk with You this day. Amen.

THE LAMB OF GOD

> The next day John seeth Jesus coming unto him, and saith, Behold the Lamb of God, which taketh away the sin of the world. *(John 1:29)*

How shall we say in a few words that which springs up in our hearts and would break forth from our lips? "The Lamb which bears away our sin" is a better rendering, for He takes it away by *bearing* it. He *bore* the sins of those who received Him while here on the earth and He bore them *away* when He paid the penalty on the cross and shed His atoning blood. *God's* Lamb! No one else could be God's Lamb. He was the *voluntary* offering. What can we do? Believe it, accept it, take our place with Him.

Let us behold You every day—Jesus, Lamb of God—counting nothing too good to give to You or too much to do for You. Amen.

THE SON OF GOD

And I saw, and bare record that this is the Son of God. *(John 1:34)*

John the Baptist had not known Him as the Messiah although he did know Him to be Mary's Son. But when the Holy Spirit descended upon Jesus at His baptism, John knew Him as the Son of God and bore record to that fact. The testimony of John the Baptist is clear! Jesus is God's Son. He is the Promised One. Not *a* Son of God, as some of our learned critics condescendingly say, but *the* Son of God. We should seek to be like John the Baptist—a sign-post pointing to Him and saying, "Behold! The Son of God." John laid down his life for his loyalty to the Son of God. May we be willing to suffer anything so that our testimony shall be clear and clean always for Him.

Lord, help us to point someone to You today and like John the Baptist to prepare the way of the Lord in all we do. Amen.

RABBI

Nathanael answered and saith unto him, Rabbi, thou art the Son of God; thou art the King of Israel. *(John 1:49)*

"Rabbi" means "teacher" and is used seven times in the New Testament. Nathanael recognized Christ as a teacher and He was—the greatest Teacher that ever lived. A careful study of the four gospels with a view to learning how Christ taught, His method, His manner, and His purpose, is better than any other possible training for Bible teachers. Christ was a true teacher. He taught the truth. He was able to make Himself understood to men of low estate. He used words which men could comprehend. He illustrated His messages in a practical manner. "The common people heard Him gladly." That was a high compliment indeed.

Lord, help us to teach by our lips and by our life. Let us pray that we may so teach today. Amen.

THE KING OF ISRAEL

> Nathanael answered and saith unto him, Rabbi, thou art the
> Son of God; thou art the King of Israel. *(John 1:49)*

When Philip found Nathanael, the latter said to him, "Can any
good thing come out of Nazareth?" But when Nathanael came
in touch with Jesus he broke out in testimony to His deity and
His messiahship. Our Lord did not fail to acknowledge this
sterling testimony, and a great promise was given to Nathanael, "Hereafter ye shall see heaven open, and the angels of
God ascending and descending." Angels were to be seen by
him. Prayers were to ascend in the name of Christ and answers were to come back through Christ. We also can see the
open heavens if we have faith.

*Lord, we send up our prayers today in Your name and
look for the answer. Amen.*

GOD'S ONLY BEGOTTEN SON

> For God so loved the world, that he gave his only begotten
> Son, that whosoever believeth in him should not perish, but
> have everlasting life. *(John 3:16)*

Here is the most beloved verse in the Bible. What a revelation
of God, of Christ, of the depths and power of love! How could
He? Abraham gave his son, and God graciously gave him
back. But *God's Son*—the Son of His love—the Only Begotten
One—was given to a lost world, to sinful men. How did He
give Him? Clothed in human form—a man! Oh, the wonders
of such a love! How it should stir our hearts! How we should
love God for His gift! How we should love our Lord Jesus
Christ—"God's Only Begotten Son"!

*Lord, help us with hearts throbbing for a lost world to go
forth today, and all the days, to tell the story to sinful, suffering men. Amen.*

THE GIFT OF GOD

> Jesus answered and said unto her, If thou knewest the gift of God, and who it is that saith to thee, Give me to drink; thou wouldest have asked of him, and he would have given thee living water. *(John 4:10)*

Here is that wonderful scene at the well of Samaria. The Lord has gone out of His way to meet the poor, sinful woman who has come to the well at a time when other women would not come; heavy-hearted, hopeless, but *One* loved her with a holy love. He is there and reveals Himself as "the Gift of God." He is God's gift to us. What is our gift to Him? May we yield ourselves and all that we are and have to Him!

Lord, help us to imitate the Samaritan woman as she went forth with the message: Come, see a man—God's gift. Amen.

MESSIAH

> The woman said unto him, I know that Messias cometh, which is called Christ: when he is come, he will tell us all things. *(John 4:25)*

There is no book like the Bible, and there never can be. Christ's interview with the woman at the well and His revelation of himself is unique and contrary to any conception that could have been made of Him. The Samaritans, as well as the Jews, anticipated a Christ (an Anointed One). This was the promise given in Deuteronomy 18:18. This woman was the last one we would have chosen for such a revelation—but her soul was filled at once with the Spirit of life and hope, and her lips bore a testimony—humiliating to herself, but bringing salvation to a multitude. Oh, that our lips might bear such convincing, convicting, and converting testimony.

Lord, make us like this Samaritan woman! May we drink deeply of the well of salvation and share the living water with others. Amen.

THE CHRIST, THE SAVIOUR OF THE WORLD

> We have heard him ourselves, and know that this is indeed the Christ, the Saviour of the world. *(John 4:42)*

The testimony of one woman brings forth from the lips of many this title, "Christ, the Saviour of the world." For two days, Christ tarried in the little city of the Samaritans and blessed fruits were harvested to His glory. These people, unlike the Jews, asked for no signs, no miracles. They took Him at His word, just as we must do. When He speaks, it is God who speaks. "We have heard Him ourselves." The need of the world today is the experience of believers manifested in a devotion to Christ and in personal testimony to a hungry-hearted world.

O Christ, Saviour of the world, baptize us with the spirit of service for You! Amen.

THE BREAD OF LIFE

> And Jesus said unto them, I am the bread of life: he that cometh to me shall never hunger; and he that believeth on me shall never thirst. *(John 6:35)*

Answering humanity's cry as embodied in the request, "Lord, evermore give us this bread," Jesus says, "I am the Bread of Life," i.e., the Life-eternal-giving Bread. This reply settles the question forever. He is the *true Bread,* the *Bread of God,* and the *Bread of life.* How is this Bread to be dispensed? It must be made known to an ignorant world. The terms upon which it is to be received must be made clear and definite. "Come to Me," says Jesus, "And you shall never hunger. Believe in Me and you shall never thirst." How simple! The "life gift" is a *love* gift. Never put a straw in the way of a hungry sinner. There is nothing to do but to believe—receive—accept. Nothing more.

Lord, help us to go out laden with the Bread of Life and give it to the hungry. Let us not give food that does not satisfy. Amen.

THE LIGHT OF THE WORLD

> Then spake Jesus again unto them, saying, I am the light of the world: he that followeth me shall not walk in darkness, but shall have the light of life. *(John 8:12)*

And God said, "Let there be light; and there was light." And "God divided the light from the darkness." Now our Lord says, "I am the Light of the world." The world is a dark, gloomy place, but "God is Light and in Him is no darkness at all." If we follow Him we shall not walk in darkness. "Walking in the light," we have fellowship with one another and reflect the glory of His person in the gloom of the world. "Arise, shine, for your light is come and the glory of the Lord is risen upon you." He can only be manifested through the lives of His own and the light of the Word.

O Lord of Light, shine in our hearts and through our lives. Amen.

I AM

> Jesus said unto them, Verily, verily, I say unto you, Before Abraham was, I am. *(John 8:58)*

The life of Abraham was limited. We know the time of his birth and of his departure. But there is no time limit to the life of our Lord. "Before Abraham was, I am." He was the Eternal Son of God. He was the Uncreated One, the Eternal One, the Self-existent One. Before the creation of the world He was the "I Am!" After the world passes away He will still be the "I Am." Without Him nothing was made that was made. He was God! Wonder of wonders! God manifest in the flesh! God pleading with men! God on the cross! God in the glory and coming in the clouds! Great is the mystery of God!

Son of God, Son of man, at the right hand of the Glory, we bow in Your presence and say with deepest reverence, "Hallowed be Your name." Amen.

THE DOOR OF THE SHEEP

> Then said Jesus unto them again, Verily, verily, I say unto you, I am the door of the sheep. *(John 10:7)*

What contrast could be greater than that between the "I Am" and this title, "Door of the Sheep"? Here our Lord paints a picture and uses an allegory into which sheep, sheepfold, and shepherd are introduced. He, Himself, claimed a peculiar position, "The Door of the sheep." He is the door by which entrance is gained to heaven. "By Me if any man enter in, he shall be saved." Put your hand upon the door—Jesus Christ on the cross—and enter the fold. There is safety. There is liberty. There is food for the sheep, and water and rest. Free from Satan's snare, filled with joy and peace, what more could we ask or desire?

Dear Lord, shepherd us today in Your own arms. Amen.

Gate for the sheep - NIV

THE GOOD SHEPHERD

> I am the good shepherd: the good shepherd giveth his life for the sheep. *(John 10:11)*

We shall have several meditations on our Lord as Shepherd, but here He speaks of Himself as the *"Good* Shepherd." God is good and Jesus is God. Therefore, He is good. If we could stop for a few moments and sense His presence, longing to speak to us in tones of deepest love, with His wonderful eyes fixed upon us, and His holy desire to draw us in loving tenderness to Himself—would we not say of Him, "He is so good. He died for me." And would not our hearts go out in passionate love to Him?

Loving Shepherd, help us to keep close to You today. Amen.

THE RESURRECTION

Jesus saith unto her, I am the resurrection, and the life: he that believeth in me, though he were dead, yet shall he live. *(John 11:25)*

Here our Lord links His own title "I Am" with the resurrection, "I am the gift of the resurrection to all who believe on me. Though he die, whoever believes on Me, yet shall he live." Faith in Him equals eternal life and that assures our resurrection. Because He lives, we *must* live. Death may come to us, but it will be the shadow only, which will pass and leave us in the full sunlight of eternal life. He who raised up Christ from the dead shall quicken our bodies. In His resurrection He conquered death. Praise the Lord!

Lord Jesus, come quickly and change these bodies of our low natural state into the likeness of Your own glorified body. Amen.

A GRAIN OF WHEAT

And Jesus answered them, saying, The hour is come, that the Son of man should be glorified. Verily, verily, I say unto you, Except a corn (grain) of wheat fall into the ground and die, it abideth alone: but if it die, it bringeth forth much fruit. *(John 12:23–24)*

A grain of wheat is so small that it can hardly be held between the fingers without dropping, and yet it is associated with His glory. He must die in order to bring forth fruit. So must we, if we are to be like Him. How hard it seems to human pride to become as a grain of wheat and then to die to this world. But listen to the words of His testimony and look upon His example. Do we desire to be like Him?

Lord, help us to ponder upon this truth today and long to be more like You. Let us be buried to our own desires in order to rise again. Amen.

A kernel of wheat - NIV

97

MASTER

Ye call me Master and Lord: and ye say well, for so I am.
(John 13:13)

"Master" means "teacher," and an authoritative Teacher He
was and is. We are to learn of Him, for He is the Truth and He
reveals the truth to men. He has left to us His words of wisdom, and we are to sit at His feet and learn of Him. We recognize this position of our Lord by yielding submission to His
authority and acknowledging it daily. He knows the past. He
knows the present. He knows the future. Let our prayer be,

"Lord, teach us Your will, through Your Word. Help us to
know, understand, and gladly live out Your will." Amen.
Teacher - NIV

THE WAY

Jesus saith unto him, I am the way. *(John 14:6)*

He is the Way—"a Way without deviation"—the straight and
narrow Way, the only Way that leads directly to the Father.
There are a thousand ways that lead to destruction, to eternal
darkness and separation from the Father. Satan has multiple
agents pointing to his wicked way, but Christ is the Sign Post,
saying; "This is the Way; walk in it." When we walk in "the
Way" we walk in the light. We journey with Him in sweet fellowship. What a joyful journey! The Way is lightened by His
countenance. He holds us by the hand. He supplies our
needs. What a Saviour!

Lord, help us to keep in touch with You as we travel along
the heavenly highway to the home prepared for us by You.
Amen.

THE TRUTH

Jesus saith unto him, I am . . . the truth. *(John 14:6)*

He is not only the Way, but He is the *Truth*—"the truth without any contradiction." We are God's free men, for we know Him who is the Truth, and the Truth makes us free. He is the Truth about the Word of God. Hear Him say, "I am not come to destroy the law or the prophets, but to fulfill." And "It is easier for heaven and earth to pass away than for one jot or tittle of the law to fail." Pity the poor deceived students in the schools and the devil-deluded ministers and teachers who cast any erroneous reflection upon the Word of God to which Jesus has set His eternal seal! Doubt concerning the inerrancy of the Bible is a doubt concerning Himself. Do not taint your soul with such unholy thoughts.

Lord, You are the Truth. We look to You. Guide us into the Truth all the days and help us to honor the perfection of Your Word. Amen.

THE LIFE

Jesus saith unto him, I am . . . the life. *(John 14:6)*

He is not only the Way and the Truth, but He is the Life—Eternal Life, the Author of Life and the Giver of Life. We almost stagger when we confront this statement by the One who left heaven and the throne of God and came to this earth that He might reveal Himself and receive to Himself those who were to inherit through Him and share with Him this eternal Life. Our short pilgrimage here is soon ended and then, O joy, we enter the unending, eternal Life.

Lord, how we thank You that You are our eternal Life through the indwelling Holy Spirit. Give us this life abundantly, even today. Amen.

THE VINE

> I am the vine, ye are the branches: He that abideth in me, and I in him, the same bringeth forth much fruit: for without me ye can do nothing. *(John 15:5)*

Here the Lord calls Himself "The Vine" as He associates Himself with the branches. He is the root and stem upon which we, as branches, must depend. The purpose of the Vine is to bear fruit. The life is in the *vine,* but that life is also in the branches, and we are to be fruit-bearing branches. "He that *abides* in Me and I in him, that same brings forth much fruit." We can bear no fruit of ourselves. Our dependence is upon Him. The desire of the Husbandman is to produce fruit, and we must ask ourselves the question: "Am I a fruit-bearing branch? If not, why not?" How patient He is, yet how fearful is the contemplation of the thought: "I may be a fruitless branch."

Lord, forbid that it should be so. Holy Spirit, fill us with Yourself that we may bear much fruit. Prune from us that which is already dead. Amen.

THE OVERCOMER

> I have overcome the world. *(John 16:33)*

A graphic picture—one of the "last night messages" of our Lord—filled with tremendous interest to every believer. A world of tribulation confronted Him and a world of tribulation confronts His church. "You shall have tribulation," and we do, but in Him we have peace—the peace of God, which passes understanding. How blessed to be in Him who is the Source of our strength! We must learn to overcome through Him. There is nothing too hard for Him. He loves to give us victory. We please Him by trusting Him and taking by faith what He has purchased for us.

Lord, we bow in Your presence and commit all to You for victory today and thus glorify our Overcomer. Amen.

OUR KEEPER

> While I was with them in the world, I kept them in thy name: those that thou gavest me I have kept. *(John 17:12)*

This prayer on the night before Christ's crucifixion is one of sacred sweetness and comfort. While He was here He guarded and kept His own. Now He is in the glory and still guards and keep us. The enemy, Satan, who captured and controlled Judas, would separate us, if he could, from our Lord; but He is "our Keeper" and we can trust in His unfailing promise: "I will keep him in perfect peace whose mind is stayed on me because he trusts in me." The enemy has ten thousand agents seeking to spoil our lives, but nothing can separate us from the love of God as manifested in Christ Jesus our Lord.

"Now unto Him who is able to keep us from falling . . . to the only wise God, our Saviour, be glory, forever." Keep us in the world but not of it. Amen.

Protector - NIV

THE SENT OF THE FATHER

> As thou hast sent me into the world, even so have I also sent them into the world. *(John 17:18)*

From the glory which He had with the Father before the world was, He was sent into this world of sin and shame to redeem sinful men. He was God's apostle—God's "Sent One." His prayer now to the Father is that they might be *sanctified* (set apart) for the great work of saving men as He was set apart for the work of redemption. This prayer was for us, also. He says, "Neither pray I for these alone, but for them also which shall believe on me through their word" (v. 20). His holy desire is that we might be in the world with the same message He had.

Lord Jesus, help us to recognize today Your call and our calling to save souls. Though we are not of the world, send us into it. Amen.

THE MAN

Behold the man. *(John 19:5)*

"Behold the man!" How little Pilate knew what he was doing when he bestowed upon our Lord that significant title, "The Man!" The word "man" is used nearly three thousand times in the Bible, but there is only one "The Man"—the Man from heaven. The word in the original is "anthropos"—a human being—and such He was. Oh, the marvel of it! It seems too good to be true, and yet it is true. For our sakes—in order to be one with us and to bear our sin—He threw aside His royal garment and donned the garments of humanity, that He might disclose to us the purpose of the Father.

In the name of this Man, we ask for guidance today and pray that our hearts may be in tune with His. Amen.

MY LORD AND MY GOD

And Thomas answered and said unto him, My Lord and my God. *(John 20:28)*

Thomas is the doubting disciple. He loved His Lord and had been willing to die with Him, but he could not believe in His bodily resurrection. He demanded a definite proof. Eight days have passed when he is confronted with the risen Jesus who says, "Put your finger in my hands, and put your hand in my side; and be not faithless but believing." Out of a heart throbbing with joy Thomas cries, "My Lord and my God." How sympathetically loving is our Lord with our unbelief. How patient He is, yet how He longs for our unquestioning, implicit faith. Let us honor Him by believing Him with all our heart.

Our Lord and our God, help us today to look upon the wounds which You carry for us and with full faith renew our pledge of loyalty to You. Amen.

A MAN APPROVED OF GOD

> Jesus of Nazareth, a man approved of God among you by miracles and wonders and signs, which God did by him in the midst of you. *(Acts 2:22)*

This is the testimony of Peter, the fisherman-apostle, concerning our Lord, Jesus of Nazareth. "A Man approved of God!" He professed to be the promised Messiah, the Son of God, and He made good His profession by His public life. His miraculous works were proof of miraculous power. He was God in human form. He set His followers the example for holy living. When believers are anointed of the Holy Spirit and seek by words and life to honor their Lord, the approval of God the Father will be upon them.

Lord, help us to live a life approved of God, so that through us wonders may be done in the salvation of souls. Amen.

A man accredited by God - NIV

GOD'S HOLY ONE

> Because thou wilt not leave my soul in hell, neither wilt thou suffer thine Holy One to see corruption. *(Acts 2:27)*

The Godhead and manhood were united in Christ, and it was impossible that He should be held by the power of death. He passed through the agony; He paid the penalty; He suffered the separation; but death could not hold Him. The unfailing Word of God had promised His resurrection and so "up from the grave He arose." He has broken the bars of death from us and in the freedom of the new life, with glorified bodies, we will be forever with Him.

May our souls be led to magnify You, the Holy One, this day and rejoice in the hope of soon being with You. Thank You that we will not see corruption. Amen.

THE PRINCE OF LIFE

> And killed the Prince of life, whom God hath raised from the dead; whereof we are witnesses. *(Acts 3:15)*

"The Prince of Life"—a remarkable title to give to our Lord when viewed in contrast to Barabbas, the murderer who took life. One—the bestower of life; the other—the destroyer of life. He came that men might have life and life more abundantly. How many there are who ignore and reject Him and who will never have the joy of living and reigning with Him through the eternal ages. Are we doing our best to make Him known to lost men?

Lord Jesus, Prince of Life, stir our hearts with compassion for the lost, and help us today to make You known to some blinded soul. Amen.
The author of life - NIV

GOD'S HOLY CHILD JESUS

> For of a truth against thy holy child Jesus, whom thou has anointed, both Herod, and Pontius Pilate, with the Gentiles, and the people of Israel, were gathered together. *(Acts 4:27)*

Peter and John were examined by the council about the healing of the lame man. They gave their testimony that this had been done in the despised name of Jesus Christ of Nazareth. The council could do nothing but let them go. Peter and John went at once to the place where the church was gathered together and reported what had been done, and the members of the assembly lifted their voices in thanksgiving. They glorified the name of the "Holy Child Jesus," against whom His enemies were gathered, and prayed that in His name signs and wonders might be manifested. Their prayer was answered.

Lord Jesus, we thank You that Your miracles are being completed today and will be until You come again. Amen.
Holy servant Jesus - NIV

A PRINCE AND A SAVIOUR

Him hath God exalted with His right hand to be a Prince and a Saviour. *(Acts 5:31)*

Here is a picture and a theme for our meditation. A convict—a criminal in the sight of men—hanging on a cross, dying an awful death of shame, suffering the agonies of hell itself that the questions of sinful man's sin might be settled forever—exalted by God to the highest heights—a Prince! But to establish His title He became the sin-bearer that He might become the sin-blotter. Destined to deepest depths of human suffering and humility, but raised to the highest heights of honor and glory. Oh, the wretchedness of our sin which demanded it, and the wonders of a Saviour who delivered it!

Lord Jesus, our Prince and our Saviour, we yield ourselves to You with glad hearts. Amen.

THE JUST ONE

Which of the prophets have not your fathers persecuted? and they have slain them which shewed before the coming of the Just One; of whom ye have been now the betrayers and murderers. *(Acts 7:52)*

The words "Just (righteous) One" burst from the lips of Stephen, the first martyr, in the wonderful message which he gave before the council in defending the name and glory of our Lord Jesus Christ. He paid with his life for his loyalty to his Lord, and he will receive his reward. It was through his testimony that the Spirit of God brought conviction to Saul of Tarsus, resulting in his conversion. How much would *we* be willing to suffer for Him?

O blessed Saviour of our souls, warm our hearts in devotion to You. Make us sturdy and strong as defenders of the faith. Amen.

The Righteous One - NIV

LORD JESUS

And they stoned Stephen, calling upon God, and saying, Lord Jesus, receive my spirit. *(Acts 7:59)*

Stephen is passing through the fire of Jewish hatred. But God is faithful to His faithful servant and martyr and opens the heavens to him, showing him Jesus standing at the right hand of His glory. The cry of Stephen was "Lord Jesus, receive my spirit." His prayer was like that of Jesus who said, "Father, into thy hands I commend my spirit" (Luke 23:46). What a testimony to the deity of our Lord! Only He who gave the spirit could receive it. To depart and be with Christ was far better for Stephen, and it will be for us when in His own good time He calls us.

Lord Jesus, help us to make a good confession, gladly facing any foe, even death that, like Stephen, we may glorify You whether in life or death. Amen.

LORD OF ALL

The word by which God sent unto the children of Israel, preaching peace by Jesus Christ: (he is Lord of all). *(Acts 10:36)*

Jesus Christ is Lord of all men. Peter was a Jew and did not want to depart from Jewish tradition, but God sent him a vision from heaven to make clear to him that He was no respecter of persons. "While Peter yet spoke the Holy Ghost fell upon all that heard the Word." Our Lord loves all; He died for all; He commissions us to go and preach to all. The world is the field, and every soul living has a claim upon us, which we must meet and answer for. What a wonderful Lord of all! What a marvelous gospel! What a rich salvation!

O Lord of all, reprove us today for our selfishness, our lack of obedience to You, and fill us with the Holy Ghost that we may gladly be witnesses to all men. Amen.

THAT MAN WHOM HE HAS ORDAINED

> Because he hath appointed a day, in which he will judge the
> world in righteousness by that man whom he hath ordained.
> *(Acts 17:31)*

Jesus was ordained—set apart, appointed, designated—as
the Man who is to judge the whole human race, and the evidence, or proof, of this is the fact of His resurrection from the
dead. It will be a righteous judgment by a righteous Judge. It
will be an impartial judgment by the One who created all
things and who knows all things, a holy, unerring Judge. He
will have the books opened before Him, and there can never
be any appeal from the verdict. What is your relation to this
Ordained Man? Are you ready?

Lord, help us to be faithful witnesses. Help us to order our
affairs and be purged of all to prepare for that day. Amen.

The man he has appointed - NIV

JESUS OF NAZARETH

> And I answered, Who art thou, Lord? And he said unto me, I
> am Jesus of Nazareth, whom thou persecutest. *(Acts 22:8)*

More than twenty times in the Scriptures is our Lord called
"Jesus of Nazareth." This is a remarkable instance. Paul is
telling the story of his conversion. He says that the words
which came to him from the heavens were "Saul, Saul, why
do you persecute Me?" And in answer to his question, "Who
are You, Lord?" came the answer, "I am Jesus of Nazareth."
That is His name *now.* Even from glory He acknowledges His
earthly title—"Jesus of Nazareth." Jesus is God. He made the
worlds, but He acknowledges the little obscure town of Nazareth, His "home town" down here.

Jesus of Nazareth, we want to be one with You. Guide us
to Your glory. We have earthly origins and duties but our citi-
zenship is in heaven. Amen.

THE FIRSTBORN AMONG MANY BRETHREN

> For whom he did foreknow, he also did predestinate to be conformed to the image of his Son, that he might be the firstborn among many brethren. *(Romans 8:29)*

A wonderful title for our Lord, "The Firstborn"! Adam was the firstborn among men, but he forfeited his rights and privileges through sin, and God ordained another Man to be the First, who was to be born of a woman, and to be the Head of a great company of brethren. God has plans for the human race and He is carrying them out as the years come and go. Jesus is the *"First*-born" and we who are "born-again" ones are, by His grace, being conformed to His image. When He comes from heaven, we will be among the sons of God united forever to and with Him.

Our eyes are fastened upon You, Firstborn One, today, and we say from our hearts, come quickly. Thank You for the new birth. Amen.

GOD'S OWN SON

> He that spared not his own Son, but delivered him up for us all, how shall he not with him also freely give us all things? *(Romans 8:32)*

"His Own Son," "His Only Son," "The Son of His Love"—the dearest, the best He gave, out of His great heart freely, lovingly, once for all to the sinful children of men. Having given us His best, will He withhold anything from us? Why do we doubt Him? Why do we live such poor, selfish, sordid lives, when the world is so needy, when hearts are so heavy and broken? Why do we fail to appropriate what He has so freely offered us? Is there not a challenge to us here? Let us meet it today.

Lord, help us to believe and with joyful hearts ask for great things for a needy world in the name of Your Son. Amen.

GOD BLESSED FOREVER

Whose are the fathers, and of whom as concerning the flesh Christ came, who is over all, God blessed for ever. Amen. *(Romans 9:5)*

As we journey through the Word of God Christ illumines it all with His presence. His titles are many. How significant is this "God blessed forever"! The promised Messiah of the Jewish stock and the flower of its race, yet they would not receive Him. He was the Shekinah glory tabernacling in human form in the midst of the world. But their eyes were blinded. What centuries of sorrow have followed and will follow until He comes for His own, and then will come the saddest of all experiences for them. Pity both Jew and Gentile in our own day who refuse to acknowledge Him as "God blessed forever."

We bow to You today and say from our hearts, "To us You are indeed 'God blessed forever.'" Amen.

THE LORD

For whosoever shall call upon the name of the Lord shall be saved. *(Romans 10:13)*

The Master loves to hear the call of a sinner for salvation. How many sin-sick, weary souls there are who have false ideas about Christ and about salvation. They would gladly cry to the Lord, but He has not been revealed to them. They need someone to tell them of His longing to have them in His family. "Faith comes by hearing and hearing by the Word of God." Listen to the words, "How beautiful are the feet of them that preach the gospel of peace and bring glad tidings of good things." "To preach" means "to tell out," "to proclaim." If you are a believer then you are a God-ordained preacher and will be held accountable for your ministry.

O Lord, our Master, send us out today to tell the love story to others. Many weary souls need Your message. Amen.

THE DELIVERER

And so all Israel shall be saved: as it is written, there shall
come out of Sion the Deliverer, and shall turn away
ungodliness from Jacob. *(Romans 11:26)*

Here we face a startling prophecy. The ancient people of
God, who at the time this book of the Bible was written were
scattered about in every land without a country of their own
except as certain permission was given them—as now to re-
side in the old land—these Jews are yet to be delivered and
as a nation they shall turn to Christ as their Deliverer and
shall be God's earthly people as we shall be His heavenly
people.

*O Lord Jesus, You have been our Deliverer. We glory in
Your name. Help us to help others to know You. Amen.*

LORD BOTH OF THE DEAD AND THE LIVING

For to this end Christ both died, and rose, and revived, that he
might be Lord both of the dead and living. *(Romans 14:9)*

Christ is the center of all affairs related to this earth. He rules.
He reigns. He keeps books, and some day those books are to
be opened. Adam and Eve and everyone who has ever lived
will be there to answer to the call. Saints (or saved ones) will
be judged for their manner of living. That will be one judgment. Sinners will be judged, and that will be another judgment. There can be no evasions, no exception. All accounts
must be faced and settled. Men should live in that prospect.
How blessed for those whose sins are covered by the blood!
But how sorrowful for even those if they have not sought to
do their best for Him!

*O Lord, may the words of our mouths and the thoughts of
our hearts be pleasing to You this day. Amen.*

MINISTER OF THE CIRCUMCISION

Now I say that Jesus Christ was a minister of the circumcision for the truth of God, to confirm the promises made unto the fathers. *(Romans 15:8)*

Here again we have a title which unites in the Spirit both Jew and Gentile as partakers of the grace of God. Christ came to the Jews with His message of love, but they would not have Him. He turned to the Gentiles and some received Him. The Gospel of Jesus Christ is for all men, because all have sinned. He came for all. He loved all. He died for all. He longs to gather all unto Himself. He is the "Minister of the Circumcision" and the "Minister of the Cross." We are one in Him.

O blessed One, minister unto us today and help us to minister unto You. May our hearts be circumcised and dedicated to You. Amen.

THE POWER OF GOD

But unto them which are called, both Jews and Greeks, Christ the power of God. *(1 Corinthians 1:24)*

When we think of possessing great power, we encounter a strange sensation. Adrenaline pumps through our beings and we think of might and authority. So when we think of our Lord Jesus Christ we can visualize Him as the Mighty One. From a power-house the electric current comes forth and darkness is displaced by light; the engine is imbued with life and moves the train carrying the armies of a nation. So our Lord Jesus Christ is the "Power of God," for all power is committed unto Him. He speaks and it is done! And this Powerful One has said, "Ask and you shall receive." How wonderful that He should love such creatures as ourselves!

Lord Jesus, we commend ourselves to You today and rest in faith in the power of Your love for us. Help us to use power wisely. Amen.

THE WISDOM OF GOD

> But unto them which are called, both Jews and Greeks,
> Christ . . . the wisdom of God. *(1 Corinthians 1:24)*

To those who are called He is "The Wisdom of God." The Bible teaches us that wisdom is a principal need and, therefore, we should seek wisdom and Him who is the storehouse of wisdom. "Never man spake like this Man." "If any man lack wisdom, let him ask in faith, nothing wavering." "Giving does not impoverish Him." "The wisdom of the world is foolishness with Him." Then let us be wise and seek the wisdom that passes all understanding.

Lord, as we face the duties and privileges of this day, guide us by Your wisdom to Your praise and glory. Amen.

RIGHTEOUSNESS

> But of him are ye in Christ Jesus, who of God is made unto
> us . . . righteousness. *(1 Corinthians 1:30)*

Righteousness is "rightness." We were all wrong and always wrong, but in Him we are made right. All of our righteousness was as filthy rags. There was nothing in us that would commend us to God and never could be. But what a change when we are in Him and He is in us. We are made sinless, *in Him,* for He bore all our sins and paid all the penalty, and His righteousness is imputed to us. What a joy to be *consciously* in Him! And what a price He paid in order to become our righteousness!

Lord, teach us to recognize this day our unworthiness and to dwell much upon the fact that You are our righteousness. Amen.

SANCTIFICATION

But of him are ye in Christ Jesus, who of God is made unto us . . . sanctification. *(1 Corinthians 1:30)*

To be "sanctified" is to be "separated"—"set apart." We could never be sanctified by our own efforts, for we are absolutely helpless except as You, Lord, become all things to us. We are in Christ Jesus and what He is, we are, and what He has, we share. We are nothing. Christ is everything. O Lord, help us to see ourselves in Christ Jesus. You have set us apart to be Your representatives in a lost world. In every act and deed we represent You.

Lord, today, may the words of our mouths and the meditations of our hearts, be acceptable unto You. Amen.

Holiness - NIV

REDEMPTION

But of him are ye in Christ Jesus, who of God is made unto us . . . redemption. *(1 Corinthians 1:30)*

What an awful thing is sin, and "coming short of the glory of God" is what sin truly is. How can any sensible person ever conceive of the possibility of a soul living with God with a sinful nature? The grace of God is wonderful. He loved us. He gave His Son for our redemption, and that Son poured out His lifeblood to atone for our sins. Who could measure the height or depth, or length or breadth of such love? Shall we not prove our love by yielding all that we are and have to Him?

Our blessed Lord, help us to walk in the light of Your love this day as the redeemed of the Lord. Amen.

THE LORD OF GLORY

> Which none of the princes of this world knew: for had they
> known it, they would not have crucified the Lord of glory.
> *(1 Corinthians 2:8)*

What a title is this! In the background are the eternal years
which the mind of man can never penetrate. "The Lord of
Glory"—Creator of all things, in whom is wrapped up all wisdom and power. "Had they known!" Oh, the pity that eyes are
closed and hearts bolted against the revelation of our Lord
who descended from the heights of glory and went into the
depths of human sorrow and suffering in order to reveal Himself to sinful men. Pity the poor princes of this world who resist His entreaties to receive Him as Saviour and Lord.

*O gracious Lord, make our meditations of You sweet this
day. Your glory is hard to comprehend. Give us grace to comprehend it. Amen.*

THE FOUNDATION

> For other foundation can no man lay than that is laid, which
> is Jesus Christ. *(1 Corinthians 3:11)*

Here we have a wonderful title for our Lord—"Jesus Christ,
the Foundation." That Foundation was laid before the world
was created. There is no other. Upon this Foundation is built
all of the purposes of God for time and for eternity. Upon it is
being built the church, "a holy temple," and a "habitation of
God through the Spirit." How is this structure to be built? By
the Holy Spirit through His own beloved disciples who are
endued and endowed with power to go into the world and
gather the stones of human souls. What a wonderful work is
assigned to us, working in harmony with Himself.

*Dear Lord, be with us this day as we seek to gather to You
precious souls who shall become stones in Your temple.
Make us also a fitting temple of Your Spirit. Amen.*

OUR PASSOVER

Purge out therefore the old leaven, that ye may be a new lump, as ye are unleavened. For even Christ our passover is sacrificed for us. *(1 Corinthians 5:7)*

The Jews had their Passover which commemorated their flight from Egypt which God accomplished with a "stretched out arm." It was a foretaste of our Passover—a Lamb without blemish, slain for our sins, whose blood sprinkled upon our hearts cleanses from sin, and whose broken body feeds our souls. With us it is a daily feast. By it we are separated from the worldly Egypt and safe forevermore. Therefore, let us keep the feast with the unleavened bread of sincerity and truth.

Lord Jesus, in sweet fellowship we would sit at Your feet and feast upon You, this day. By Your blood we have passed over from death to life. Amen.

THAT SPIRITUAL ROCK

And did all drink the same spiritual drink: for they drank of that spiritual Rock that followed them: and that Rock was Christ. *(1 Corinthians 10:4)*

Paul is calling attention to the journey of the children of Israel through the wilderness and comparing it to the life of the church. They were supernaturally supplied daily with food and water. The water was a gift from God; symbolizing the Water of Life which springs from the spiritual Rock, which is Christ. He is our "Rock," and from His pierced side flow rivers of living water. How often we have sung, "Jesus the Water of Life will give, freely, freely, freely"—and then how often we have forgotten to slake our thirst from that Fountain which will never cease to flow down through the ages.

Lord Jesus, our spiritual Rock, help us to drink freely of Your living water today. Though You give freely, we need to ask in order to receive. Amen.

THE HEAD OF EVERY MAN

But I would have you know, that the head of every man is Christ. *(1 Corinthians 11:3)*

God reigns supreme in this world, but God is manifested in the flesh in the person of Jesus, who is supreme over all humanity. Every man is morally bound to acknowledge and obey His authority. He is the "Head over all things to the church." Were the church to acknowledge His authority and become obedient to His command, what a different condition would exist. As Head of the church He has given orders to "go into all the world and preach the gospel," but His command has not been obeyed. Let us bow to His agenda and let every one of us seek to do his part.

Lord Jesus, we bow to Your plans today. Help us to tell the story of the cross to a lost world. You rule as our head in all things. Amen.

THE FIRSTFRUITS OF THEM THAT SLEEP

But now is Christ risen from the dead, and become the firstfruits of them that slept. *(1 Corinthians 15:20)*

Here is an emphatic statement, "Now *is* Christ risen." There can be no controversy over this fact. The church itself is the challenge to all doubters. The Bible, the lives of believers, all witness to the fact of His resurrection. He is the "firstfruits," the beginning, and every believer looks forward with glad anticipation to the coming day of all days when the trumpet shall sound and "the dead in Christ shall rise first." This is the blessed hope—to be with Him and like Him forever.

Make this a glad day, our Lord, as we contemplate this wonderful truth and think of You as the coming, glorious One. You are the beginning of the promised eternal life. Amen.

THE LAST ADAM

> And so it is written, The first man Adam was made a living soul; the last Adam was made a quickening spirit. *(1 Corinthians 15:45)*

The *first* Adam was created out of the dust of the earth and God breathed into his nostrils the breath of life. The *last* Adam was conceived by the Holy Ghost. He was a "God-Man." The first Adam was innocent; the last Adam was holy. The first became a sinner; the second was sinless. He was a life-giving Spirit. He was the Life-giver and the Light-giver. Through this last Adam, through faith, we receive the nature that prepares us for an eternal inheritance and qualifies us for the celestial joys of the celestial city.

Our Lord, You have quickened us by the indwelling Spirit, and we meditate with grateful hearts upon You, the last Adam. We look forward to a city not made with human hands. Amen.

A QUICKENING SPIRIT

> And so it is written . . . the last Adam was made a quickening spirit. *(1 Corinthians 15:45)*

We are of the earth, earthy, by birth, but we have a new birth. That which was first was natural and earthy; afterward comes the spiritual. How wonderful is the operation of God in creating in fallen man eternal life! "He that has the Son has life." These mortal bodies shall become, through the power of our Lord as the "Quickening Spirit," glorious, immortal bodies in which He will dwell through the eternal years. What a glorious outlook for us whose eyes are turned heavenward where we look for Him.

O quickening Spirit, come quickly! We long to see You! We long to receive our glorified bodies. Amen.

A life-giving spirit - NIV

117

THE LORD FROM HEAVEN

The first man is of the earth, earthy; the second man is the Lord from heaven. *(1 Corinthians 15:47)*

The contrast here again is between Adam and Christ. Adam was of the earth. The Lord was from heaven. The first man was a failure, and all men are born in sin and are failures. Therefore, there is the necessity of a "Man from Heaven." Our eyes are fixed upon Him today—this "Second Man." All men bear the image of the earthy, but to bear the image of the heavenly, Christ should be their desire. Let us seek by holy fellowship with Him today to reflect His image in this sinful world.

Lord Jesus, help us to walk and talk with You today and put off the "old Adam," being conformed to Christ. Amen.

The second man from heaven - NIV

THE IMAGE OF GOD

In whom the god of this world hath blinded the minds of them which believe not, lest the light of the glorious gospel of Christ, who is the image of God, should shine upon them. *(2 Corinthians 4:4)*

Satan is the god of this world and the prince of the power of the air. The eyes of every unsaved person have been blinded to the vision of Christ who is the "Image of God." Their minds are on earthly things in which there is no joy, no peace, no satisfaction. Satan hates our Lord with a bitter hatred, and as the days pass and the coming of the Lord draws near, Satan's blinding powers are more and more apparent. This fact should stir our hearts to increased desire and intensified purpose to present to the unsaved Jesus, the Image of God, who is so precious to us.

Lord Jesus, fill us with Your Holy Spirit and give us a passion for the blinded souls of the unsaved. Let Your image be clearly seen in us. Amen.

GOD'S UNSPEAKABLE GIFT

Thanks be unto God for his unspeakable gift. *(2 Corinthians 9:15)*

Paul has been praising the Corinthians for their liberal gifts to the saints in Judea. His heart is full and he breaks forth in a note of praise as he thinks of God's greater gift of His Son—"Thanks for the unspeakable Gift." There was no treasure which God could give comparable to the gift of His Son, and having given us His Son, "will he not with Him freely give us all things?" How could it be possible that the Father would give to sinners the Son of His Love? How we ought to love Him! Is there anything we have or are that we would withhold from Him?

Loving Lord, help us to sense in a new way what it means for us to possess You, the unspeakable Gift. Amen.

His indescribable gift - NIV

CHRIST

Blessed be the God and Father of our Lord Jesus Christ, who hath blessed us with all spiritual blessings in heavenly places in Christ. *(Ephesians 1:3)*

Three times the word "bless" is used in this verse. God is a blessed God and He showers His blessings upon His people. What are these spiritual blessings in Christ? They are spiritual gifts, the blessings of the Gospel—the "Good News" from God. They include the eternal purpose and precious promises of God which are to be manifested now, in the future, and throughout eternity. As you read your Bible, note them. How many! They are strengthening, encouraging, satisfying, and enduring. And all *in* Christ and *only* in Him.

How we rejoice, O Christ of God, that by faith we are in You and all of Your blessings are for us. Help us to appreciate them with thankful hearts. Amen.

119

HEAD OVER ALL THINGS

And hath put all things under his feet, and gave him to be the head over all things to the church. *(Ephesians 1:22)*

The gift of God to the church—which is His body—was Christ, whom He raised from the dead and seated above all principalities and powers and might and dominion and every name which is named both in this world and in that which is to come. We need to recognize our exalted position—bone of His bone and flesh of His flesh—chosen in Him before the world was created—dear as the apple of His eye. Let us live in the enjoyment of our great privileges and in the assurance that through the endless ages we shall be His blessed, beloved ones.

O Head of the church, keep us in happy, holy, heavenly fellowship with Yourself this day, and until You do come! Let Your rule be over everything in our lives. Amen.

Head over everything - NIV

HE THAT FILLETH ALL IN ALL

Which is his body, the fullness of him that filleth all in all. *(Ephesians 1:23)*

The church is the "fullness of Christ." The church can never be complete until the last member is brought into the body. Therefore, the business of the church is to be busy seeking to save the lost. Every soul added increases His fullness. The life of Christ pulses though His body, the church, and through each individual member. Why, then, are we not filled with Christ? Because we are not yet yielded to the indwelling Holy Spirit, who imparts the life of Christ and who takes the things of Christ and shows them unto us.

Blessed Holy Spirit, give us a passion to know more and more of Him who fills all in all. Let us surrender to You in every area of our lives. Amen.

Him who fills everything in every way - NIV

OUR PEACE

For he is our peace, who hath made both one, and hath broken down the middle wall of partition between us. *(Ephesians 2:14)*

"He is our peace." Thank God, we have everything in Him. In the poor, decaying world, we have tribulations, trials, disappointments, sorrows of all kinds, but there never will be a time when we may not pillow our heads upon His shoulder and be at peace. Christ has reconciled both Jew and Gentile, and the old wall of separation is broken down. He has reconciled men with God. Remember His words that last night with His disciples: "Peace I leave with you, my peace I give unto you. . . . Let not your heart be troubled, neither let it be afraid."

Blessed Lord Christ, we look to You with glad hearts and pray that the peace of God that passes understanding may garrison our souls today. Our resting place is in You. Amen.

ONE LORD

One Lord, one faith, one baptism. *(Ephesians 4:5)*

The apostle is stating in this and the succeeding verses a great truth concerning the church. There is a seven-fold unity. One *body*—composed of believers. One *Spirit*—the Holy Spirit who dwells within every believer and unites them together in the common bond. One *hope*—the blessed hope of His coming. One *Lord*—the Lord over all. One *faith*—and that founded on the one Lord. One *baptism*—and that the baptism into Christ. One *God and Father* of all—the object of our faith and in whose name all believers are baptized. We are not our own. We were bought with a great price. We are His subjects, under His rule and authority.

Lord Jesus, let us bow to You as the one Lord, and with loyal hearts yield to Your authority. Amen.

THE HEAD

> But speaking the truth in love, may grow up into him in all things, which is the head, even Christ. *(Ephesians 4:15)*

We have already viewed Christ as the "Head over all things," but here we have Him as the Head of the body of believers—the church. There is inspiration in this thought—that we are to grow up into Him. How are we to do this? We have His life within us. The Head dominates the body, and according to the need, the supply is furnished. The new nature demands a supply that cannot come from any other source than the Head. What a wonderful body the church would be, were it always mindful of its Head and responding to His desire for it!

Lord, help us to look unto You, great Head of the church, and as members of Your body, to grow into Your likeness. Amen.

AN OFFERING

> And walk in love, as Christ also hath loved us, and hath given himself for us an offering. *(Ephesians 5:2)*

Hear Him speaking that last night: "Greater love hath no man than this, that a man lay down his life for his friends." What an offering for those disciples who deserted Him that very night! He became sin for us. He said, concerning the offering of His life, "I have power to lay it down and power to take it up." No man could take His life without His consent, who through the eternal Spirit offered Himself without spot to God.

Lord Jesus, we recognize Your offering in our behalf. Help us to walk in love as You have also loved us, and may our fellowship with You be sweet this day. Amen.

A SACRIFICE TO GOD

And walk in love, as Christ also hath loved us, and hath given himself . . . a sacrifice to God. *(Ephesians 5:2)*

God's holiness and righteousness demanded some way by which sin could be forgiven and removed, so that sinful men could have access to Him and live in fellowship with Him. There was only one way. Sin—violation of the law—must be punished, and the sinner must be justified from all things. The Law of Moses could not do this. The offerings of the Old Testament could not do it. But God had a way. So "now once in the end of the age has He appeared to put away sin by the sacrifice of Himself." "It is finished" were His words on the cross. Through His sacrifice our sins were washed away and rights and titles to Heaven granted us.

Lord, forbid that we should ever hesitate to sacrifice all for You! Let us walk in self-denial and giving to others. Amen.

A SWEETSMELLING SAVOUR

And walk in love, as Christ also hath loved us, and hath given himself . . . for a sweetsmelling savour. *(Ephesians 5:2)*

When Noah came out of the ark he took of every clean beast and of every clean fowl and offered a burnt offering unto the Lord. "And the Lord smelled a sweet savour." When Christ laid down His life on the cross what a perfume went up to God—the perfume from the sacrifice of His Son! Has the perfume of the cross yet reached you? It reached heaven. Has the love of God, as manifested in the sacrifice of His Son, mastered you?

Our Father, forgive us that we have been so unmindful of the wonders of Your love. May its perfume pervade our lives, and through us, the lives of others. Amen.

A fragrant offering - NIV

A SERVANT

> But made himself of no reputation, and took upon him the
> form of a servant, and was made in the likeness of men.
> *(Philippians 2:7)*

Isaiah spoke concerning Him: "Behold, my servant shall deal
prudently, he shall be exalted and extolled, and be very high."
"His visage was marred more than any man." The meaning of
the word *servant* is "a doer" or "a slave." Christ was God manifest in the flesh, but "He emptied Himself," made Himself of
"no reputation." Christ is the second Adam. He is the representative of perfect manhood. As a servant, He humbled Himself. From what lofty heights—Creator of all things—down to
a servant of men, step-by-step in service to receive the lashes
and the cross. What an example for us is He—the Servant!

*O Christ our Beloved, help us to follow in Your footsteps
and be in deed and in truth Your chosen servants. Amen.*

GOD'S DEAR SON

> Who hath delivered us from the power of darkness, and hath
> translated us into the kingdom of his dear Son. *(Colossians
> 1:13)*

To "His dear Son" is here attributed the deliverance and
translation of the believer from the power of Satan, the ruler
of this dark world. Millions are dwelling today, ignorant of
Him, controlled by the power of a satanic nature, resisting
His Word, and doomed to eternal darkness. There is but One
who can deliver men. It is *His dear Son.* We are the possessors of this truth and have experienced it. How can we—how
dare we—be indifferent to the blinded souls all around us
when God's dear Son is longing to have them respond to His
call, "Come unto Me"?

*O beloved Son, make us light-bearers to darkened souls
today. Amen.*

The Son he loves - NIV

THE IMAGE OF THE INVISIBLE GOD

> Who is the image of the invisible God, the firstborn of every creature. *(Colossians 1:15)*

It is difficult for us to refrain from loud acclamation as we view this expression concerning our Lord, the very "Image of the Invisible God!" We look at Him and we see God. We hear His voice and we hear God. We see Him holding the children in His arms, and we see God. We see Him in the home of friends, and we see God. We see Him feeding the multitudes, and we see God. There is but one God, and He is the One. "Great is the mystery!" Great is our expectation! Glory to God in the highest! We know Him. We love Him. We wait with longing hearts for Him.

Lord Jesus, in whom dwells all the fullness of the God-head bodily, we worship You! We adore You! We look and long for You. Amen.

THE FIRSTBORN OF EVERY CREATURE

> Who is the image of the invisible God, the firstborn of every creature. *(Colossians 1:15)*

"The firstborn of every creature," *creature* meaning "of everything made." So many statements in the Scripture make plain the fact that God and Christ are One. Christ is the manifestation of God. He unites man and God. The invisible God has become visible to men in Jesus Christ. He is the Sovereign Lord of the natural creation and of the new creation, so that He is intimately allied to us. He is the first begotten from the dead. We could write a book about it, but a Book *has* been written.

Blessed Lord, our Firstborn, to whom we are united forever, help us to glorify You today. Help us to see You clearly in Your Word, for then we see the Father. Amen.

The firstborn over all creation - NIV

125

CREATOR OF ALL THINGS

For by him were all things created. *(Colossians 1:16)*

He is the "Creator of All Things"—visible and invisible! Think a moment. Do not allow the magnitude of this revelation to escape you as your eyes are resting upon your loving Lord. Are we not prone to underestimate Him and undervalue His work? See how Paul visualizes it in Ephesians 3:8–9: "Unto me, who am less than the least of all saints, is this grace given, that I should preach among the Gentiles the unsearchable riches of Christ. And to make all men see what is the fellowship of the mystery, which from the beginning of the world has been hid in God, who created all things by Jesus Christ." Should we not take a place lower than Paul who counted himself the least of all saints?

Lord, help us. Keep ambition and pride from dominating us. Keep us at Your feet in worship and praise. Help us to realize the majesty of You, the creator of the universe. Amen.

THE HEAD OF THE BODY

And he is the head of the body, the church: who is the beginning, the firstborn from the dead; that in all things he might have the preeminence. *(Colossians 1:18)*

The Word of God emphasizes this fact over and over again, and we need to have it emphasized so that we can be always viewing Him in the proper spirit. The church is His body. We are members of that body. We are One with Him. What is involved in this? We must recognize our relationship and think of Him always as our Head and look to Him for wisdom and guidance. We must joyfully seek to walk in fellowship with Him, do His good pleasure, and in all things please Him.

Lord Jesus, great Head of the church, help us to honor You this day by words and righteous living. Let us indeed give You preeminence in everything. Amen.

THE BEGINNING

Who is the beginning, the firstborn from the dead.
(Colossians 1:18)

He is "The Beginning." Who is? The "firstborn from the dead." By His resurrection, He inaugurated a new era, the beginning of a new life—eternal life. He is the "firstfruits of them that slept," the Prince of life. He solved the problem forever. He rose from the dead. He conquered death. His resurrection assures the resurrection of the bodies of all those who sleep in Him. The mystery is solved. There can be no end to this eternal life which we have through faith in Him, for it is His life. Let us stop and meditate today upon all that it means.

Blessed Lord, who is the beginning of that life in us that is insured forever, help us to realize you are the beginning and the end. Amen.

THE FIRSTBORN FROM THE DEAD

And he is . . . the firstborn from the dead; that in all things he might have the preeminence. *(Colossians 1:18)*

Here we have the origin of Christ's headship. "He is the firstfruits of them that sleep," or "have fallen asleep." He is the originator of spiritual life, "the beginning of the new creation of God." He died and was among the dead. Through death, He paid the penalty for sin and was raised for our justification "from *among* the dead." Others were translated or were raised but died again. He rose to die no more. This resurrection guarantees His headship and assures the resurrection of all believers. He has the preeminence in all things.

Our Lord Jesus, we glorify Your name as The Firstborn from the Dead and look forward to the day when we also shall be raised and, with glorified bodies, abide with You forever. Amen.

HOPE OF GLORY

> To whom God would make known what is the riches of the glory of this mystery among the Gentiles; which is Christ in you, the hope of glory. *(Colossians 1:27)*

Here is a revelation not made known in other ages to the sons of men but now revealed by the Holy Spirit to the church. Paul is continually impressing the wonderful truth of God's will as the cause and work of salvation and the wonderful privilege bestowed upon him of preaching it. This glory which is so wonderful is the garment with which all believers will be clothed when the Christ comes for us. How we should prize the possession of "Christ in us." Do we, and do we long that others might possess it also?

Lord, give us a hunger for others that they might also be the rich possessors of the Hope of Glory. Thank You for the riches we possess through You. Amen.

CHRIST OUR LIFE

> When Christ, who is our life, shall appear, then shall ye also appear with him in glory. *(Colossians 3:4)*

Hallelujah! What a promise is this: "When He shall appear"! He shall change these bodies of our fallen nature and fashion them like His own glorious body. Our life is in Him, "For me to live is Christ." He could not appear without us. He is preparing a place for us. He is coming for us. The anticipation of this is the great incentive of our life. These mortal bodies will be clothed like His glorious body. There can be no condition in life here which can rob us of the joy of this great truth. Let us breathe this atmosphere and look forward to that glorious day when the great change shall take place.

O Lord, our Life, we will seek to honor You this day. May it be a day which pleases You through all our words and deeds. Amen.

ALL AND IN ALL

Where there is neither Greek nor Jew, circumcision nor uncircumcision, Barbarian, Scythian, bond nor free: but Christ is all and in all. *(Colossians 3:11)*

Christ is the Creator of all things. "Without Him was not anything made that was made." He is in all things. In Him we "live, and move, and have our being." He is the beginning and the end of all things. He is the criterion by which all things must be measured. All power is in Him. All dominion, all authority is vested in Him. All distinctions are swept away. There is neither Jew nor Greek, old nor young, rich nor poor, learned nor ignorant, bond nor free. He unifies all by His indwelling Holy Spirit.

Lord, help us to recognize this blessed truth that You unify all under You, to abide in it, and so to glorify You this day. Help us reach out to believers of different backgrounds. Amen.

LORD OF PEACE

Now the Lord of peace himself give you peace always by all means. The Lord be with you all. *(2 Thessalonians 3:16)*

Our Lord is the Author of peace. He came to make peace possible. "Peace I leave with you, my peace I give unto you." In order to have this wonderful peace we must be yoked up close to Himself. We live in a world of unrest and conflict. The heart of humanity beats high with excitement. "No peace for the wicked!" How we should pity them. They do not know Him. They can never know Him unless He is revealed to them. We are His spokesmen. Let us cheerfully make Him manifest today.

Lord of Peace, we pillow our heads upon Your bosom. Your peace passes understanding. We thank You. Let us make peace between You and all people. Amen.

129

OUR HOPE

Paul, an apostle of Jesus Christ, by the commandment of God our Saviour, and Lord Jesus Christ, which is our hope. *(1 Timothy 1:1)*

He is "Our Hope." His promises assure us and fix our faith upon Him. He is the center of the life of a true believer. We could not think of the coming glory without eyes fixed upon Him. The incentive of a loyal life is to please Him. What could be more satisfying after a day of toil and burden-bearing than to remember how His Word was our comfort and His promises our peace? We look at the rising sun as it bathes the mountain peaks with its glory, and at the glittering stars at night: They all foretell the coming of the glorious day when He will have us with Himself.

Lord, our Hope, our faith is fixed on You. Help us to rest upon You this day. You are an anchor to our soul. Amen.

THE MEDIATOR

For there is one God, and one mediator between God and men, the man Christ Jesus. *(1 Timothy 2:5)*

God is One and there is but one Mediator between God and man, and that is a Man; but that Man—praise God—is the Man Christ Jesus. "He is the Mediator of the New Testament" for by means of death for the redemption of men He alone is qualified to act in man's behalf. He loved us. He died for us. Christ is God, but Christ is also the Head of humanity, and He alone is capable of filling the position of Mediator. How wonderful He is, and He is all we need.

Blessed Mediator, our sin-bearer, we open our hearts to You as we confess our sins and look with satisfaction upon the blood of Your atonement. Amen.

THE MAN CHRIST JESUS

> For there is one God and one mediator between God and
> men, the man Christ Jesus. *(1 Timothy 2:5)*

We have considered Christ as mediator and now we see the
emphasis upon Christ, *our* mediator, as the man Christ Jesus.
In these days when so many rob Him of His deity, we should
rejoice in the privilege offered us of magnifying Him as both
man and God. "Great is the mystery of godliness: God was
manifest in the flesh." No picture in the Bible is so thrilling,
so calculated to convince and convert, as that of God dying
for men. See Him today—arms outstretched above a blood-
stained body, saying, "Come unto Me. I will give you rest."

*O crucified, risen God-man, we adore You. Guide us today
in our worship and work for You and help us to rest in Your
love. Amen.*

GOD MANIFEST IN THE FLESH

> And without controversy great is the mystery of godliness:
> God was manifest in the flesh, justified in the Spirit, seen of
> angels, preached unto the Gentiles, believed on in the world,
> received up into glory. *(1 Timothy 3:16)*

Here is a sermon of marvelous mystery. In a few words we are
given the magnitude of the mission of Christ in leaving the
glory and coming to this earth, clothed in the garments of
flesh; accomplishing His divine mission of redemption while
in human form; leaving His witnesses to His crucifixion, resurrection, and ascension to His high and holy place in glory.
We should stand with uncovered heads and with hearts beat-
ing in adoration, worship Him as the Holy Spirit of God emphasizes to us this great truth: He came, He died, He lives in
us, and He lives in glory; and we will dwell forever with Him.

*Holy Spirit, help us to magnify and glorify the God-man.
Help us to understand the great truths of all Your deeds. Amen.*
Appeared in a body - NIV

BLESSED AND ONLY POTENTATE

Which in his times he shall shew, who is the blessed and only Potentate, the King of kings, and Lord of lords. *(1 Timothy 6:15)*

This term is used but once in the Bible and means the "All Powerful One." Limitless power is to be manifested at His appearing who is King of kings. At this, the final event, our Lord will reveal Himself and bring with Him crowns for the victors who have waged a good warfare and stand ready to receive the promised prize, which none can dispute His authority to bestow. Paul is so overcome with this vision that he breaks forth in notes of highest acclaim (read the sixteenth verse).

O Mighty One, we unite with Your servant Paul and ascribe honor and power unto Your name and wait for Your glorious appearing. Amen.

The blessed and only Ruler - NIV

JUDGE OF THE QUICK AND THE DEAD

I charge thee therefore before God, and the Lord Jesus Christ, who shall judge the quick and the dead . . . preach the Word. *(2 Timothy 4:1–2)*

The Christian life is a serious life to live. It is stewardship for Christ, and a day of accounting must come. We must *all* appear before Him to give an account for the deeds done in the body. There is no escape from our responsibility for obedience to the command, "Preach (tell) the Word (of God); be instant in season, out of season." How critical! Every man's work will be tried by fire and judged for what it is. Gold, silver, precious stones; wood, hay, stubble! No one can change the record—neither God nor man. Are you ready?

Lord Jesus, we look for Your coming. Help us to do our best today to make Your will and Your way known. We depend totally on Your free grace. Amen.

The judge of the living and the dead - NIV

THE RIGHTEOUS JUDGE

> Henceforth there is laid up for me a crown of righteousness, which the Lord, the righteous judge, shall give me at that day. *(2 Timothy 4:8)*

In the judgment spoken of here there is a promised reward which Paul speaks of as coming to himself and to all those who love the truth concerning the coming of the Lord. They are to be crowned and the Lord will Himself put the crown upon the head of those who are true to His promises and who look for Him—a "crown of righteousness." There are many crowns awaiting the saints. Salvation is a *gift,* but crowns are for those whose lives have been lived in obedience to the Word of God. His shed blood should be the appeal to us to be willing to lay down our lives for Him.

Lord Jesus, give us an increasing desire to see You and be with You. We pray that through faith, Your grace, and obedience, we may receive the crown You prepare. Amen.

BLESSED HOPE

> Looking for that blessed hope, and the glorious appearing of the great God and our Saviour Jesus Christ. *(Titus 2:13)*

His appearing is the culmination of all our hopes. He will vanquish all sickness, sin, and death and restore all we lost in Eden. He is our glorious hope, or as Paul says, our hope of glory. He will be the culmination of all history, and His enemies will not thwart His will.

Dear Lord, let us never lose hope in Your unfailing love and Your certain victory in our world and our lives. Amen.

THE GREAT GOD

Looking for that blessed hope, and the glorious appearing of the great God and our Saviour Jesus Christ. *(Titus 2:13)*

For whom are we looking? Everywhere it is stated in the Scripture that we are to look for our Lord—for Jesus Christ who died. "This same Jesus shall so come as you have seen Him go." He will come with His glorified body; with the hands that were pierced; with the wounded side from which the lifeblood was poured out; with the scarred brow where the thorns left their marks. The same voice that said, "Behold My hands and My feet. It is I, be not afraid" will welcome us when we meet Him in the air.

Lord Jesus, we wait with expectant hearts, and our voices are tuned for the Hallelujah Chorus as we say, "Come." Come into our today and sanctify us. Amen.

HEIR OF ALL THINGS

Hath in these last days spoken unto us by his Son, whom he hath appointed heir of all things, by whom also he made the worlds. *(Hebrews 1:2)*

How logical the Bible is. To our Lord is ascribed glory because He is the Creator of all things. He made the worlds. He says, "All things that the Father has are Mine." Unlimited power is His. Unlimited possessions are His. We are also His. Praise God, what a revelation we have of Him! He purchased us with His own priceless blood. We are dear to Him as the apple of His eye. He will never leave us nor forsake us. We belong to the "Heir of all things." Our needs will be supplied, then, for we are heirs of God and joint-heirs with Jesus Christ. Let us keep our heads erect and our eyes turned heavenward.

O blessed Heir of All Things, take us under Your wings today. May we be gloriously happy in fellowship with You. Amen.

THE BRIGHTNESS OF HIS GLORY

Who being the brightness of his glory. *(Hebrews 1:3)*

Do you want to visualize the glory of God? Then gaze upon Jesus Christ. When we see Him, we see God, for He is God. Oh, the marvelous attributes of the Godhead! How wonderful it is! How fascinating is this Bible of ours in which we have such a revelation of God as manifest in the flesh! Moses prayed to God, "I beseech You, show me Your glory" and the answer was, "I will make all my goodness pass before You." With your Bible in hand, meditate upon this revelation of Jesus Christ and rejoice in Him as *your own Lord.*

Father, let the rays of sunshine from the person of Christ shine in our hearts today. May they purge away all the impurities from our hearts. Amen.

The radiance of God's glory - NIV

THE EXPRESS IMAGE OF HIS PERSON

Who being the brightness of his glory, and the express image of his person. *(Hebrews 1:3)*

"No man hath seen God at any time; the only begotten Son, which is in the bosom of the Father, he hath declared him." We have seen the Father for we have seen the Son. We have seen Him, a man among men, eating, drinking, living, working with them. When a seal is stamped upon a piece of paper, we have its exact image. When we see Jesus we see the God-man—a *perfect* representation of God, and we see the *only* God we will ever see. Hold that truth and meditate upon it for a while, and let the Holy Spirit magnify Christ to you. Thank God, we have seen Him, we know Him, we love Him, we are one with Him.

Lord, let us bask in the sunshine of Your love today. Mold and fashion us more and more in conformity to Your image. Amen.

The exact representation of his being - NIV

THE UPHOLDER OF ALL THINGS

> Who being the brightness of his glory, and the express image of his person, and upholding all things by the word of his power. *(Hebrews 1:3)*

God is Light. Jesus is the radiance of that light. God is the Sun and Jesus is the Sunbeam. The sun and sunshine are co-existent. We see the sunbeam, not the sun itself, but the rays of the sun. If you break a sunbeam through a prism, you have all the colors. When Jesus was broken on the cross, all of the richness of the glory of God was manifested. He is the express image of the person of God. He is "The Upholder of All Things." He created all things. He purged all sin. In the palm of His hand are all things. You can trust all to Him.

Lord Jesus, we thank You for Your finished work. We rest in You. Keep us trustful and faithful until Your coming. Amen.

Sustaining all things - NIV

GOD

> But unto the Son he saith, Thy throne, O God, is for ever and ever. *(Hebrews 1:8)*

Here we have the Alpine height in titles for our Lord. "Your throne, O *God!*" All other names and titles are inferior to this. When He was born in a manger, God was there. When He worked at the carpenter's trade, God was there at work. When He associated with the fishermen, it was God who was their companion. When He spoke, God spoke. When He died on the cross, it was God Himself who poured out His life. When He comes "with a shout," it will be the voice of God that calls us to be with Him forever. God the Son holds the scepter and rules the worlds, and we will rule and reign with Him.

O God, our Saviour and Coming King, hasten Your coming, and help us to help You hasten that day, for Your name's sake. Work as only You can to make us like You, God. Amen.

THE CAPTAIN OF OUR SALVATION

> For it became him . . . to make the captain of their salvation perfect through sufferings. *(Hebrews 2:10)*

We cannot but bow our heads as we read this verse and meditate upon "The Captain of Our Salvation" and His perfection. He was God and He was man, we have learned. As man He must be manifest in the life. He is the Son of God, the Captain (or "Author") of salvation. We are the *sons* of God. The mode and method of perfection is demonstrated by our Leader. He was tempted; so are we. He suffered, so must we. He was persecuted; so must we be. He paid the price; so must we. The climax for Him and for us is glory.

Lord, we bow our heads and hearts to You, our Leader, today and obey Your orders. Thank You that You have promised to be with us in every trial and suffering, our Captain throughout this life. Amen.

THE SEED OF ABRAHAM

> For verily he took not on him the nature of angels; but he took on him the seed of Abraham. *(Hebrews 2:16)*

This suggestive title surely draws a picture well worthy of our consideration. Why did He not take on Himself the nature of angels? Do not the fallen angels need help? Are they inferior to men? Will they evolve into good angels? No, but those angels who fell did so in full consciousness of all that it meant. He came to fallen man and took upon Himself the "seed of Abraham" because He longed to lift us to heights above even the angels.

Our Lord, the wonder of Your work for us astonishes us. Keep us, we pray, from being selfish. Help us to tell the story of Your love to our fellow men. Amen.

137

THE APOSTLE

Consider the Apostle and High Priest of our profession, Christ
Jesus. *(Hebrews 3:1)*

Jesus was an apostle (or "Sent One"). He was sent with the
Gospel (Good News). God sent prophets and angels to bear
His messages to men. He sent Moses, the mighty man of
God. But now we are looking at the Apostle from heaven's
court itself. He came to bring the most wonderful message
ever intended for mortal ears: "God so loved the world!" Why
did He so love it, and how was that love manifested? This
Apostle did His work and has appointed us, who are believers, to carry it on to fallen men. This Apostle was faithful. Are
we? We are His authorized representatives.

*Help us to be Your "sent ones" today, bearing the joyful
message of salvation to those who know it not. We know the
miracle of your being sent to us for salvation. Amen.*

THE BUILDER

For this man was counted worthy of more glory than Moses,
inasmuch as he who hath builded the house hath more
honour than the house. *(Hebrews 3:3)*

Christ is here set forth as "The Builder" or "Establisher" of the
house. He is the apostle. He is the High Priest. The foundation of the house is laid in Him. "You are God's building,"
Paul says in 1 Corinthians 3:9. We are temples of the Holy
Spirit now. Christ dwells within us. We are to be built up into
a holy temple from which will go forth the voices of millions
of the redeemed as they sing the Hallelujah Chorus. Let Christ
have His way in fitting us for our appointed places in the
Temple of God, for He is the Master Builder and we are to
share with Him in the coming day.

*Grant unto us, Lord, submission to Your holy will in all
things this day. Build us into the house of Your body, the
church. Amen.*

THE GREAT HIGH PRIEST

> Seeing, then, that we have a great high priest, that is passed into the heavens, Jesus the Son of God, let us hold fast our profession. *(Hebrews 4:14)*

Jesus, the Son of God, is our "Great High Priest." Where is He? In the glory, at the right hand of the glory of God. What is He there for? He is our representative. We can come with boldness to the throne of grace, and we will find grace for every need. He is the Son of God with power. He loves us. He took our place on the cross. He settled every claim against us. Satan may condemn us, but our great High Priest holds forth His pierced hands, and that is enough.

Lord Jesus, while You are representing us in the glory yonder, help us to represent You here. We need You to mediate for us as our eternal Priest. Amen.

A PRIEST FOREVER

> Thou art a priest for ever after the order of Melchisedec. *(Hebrews 5:6)*

He is our High Priest, our Great Priest, and "A Priest Forever" after the order of Melchisedec (Genesis 14:18–20), that mysterious character who typified our Lord. Will Christ be our representative throughout eternity? Yes—and *we* will be *His* representatives throughout eternity. For our new life is eternal. How it warms our hearts to think of that word "forever" in connection with our relation to Christ! He is our eternal High Priest, and we are to be kings and priests in association with Him (Revelation 1:6). We are undone, hell-deserving sinners, but through Him, we are lifted to eternal heights.

Lord, our great High Priest, help us to honor You by our words and our lives. Let us be a kingdom of priests offering You spiritual sacrifices. Amen.

AUTHOR OF ETERNAL SALVATION

> And being made perfect, he became the author of eternal
> salvation unto all them that obey him. *(Hebrews 5:9)*

Christ was perfected through suffering. He was obedient unto
death, even the death of the cross, and through the hard, cruel, sacrificial journey which He made to the cross—suffering
beyond the power of thought to comprehend—He perfected
a way by which men could be saved. When He bore our sin
on the cross, the unchanging law of God was in operation,
and He suffered separation from God. There was but one way
by which sinful men could be made righteous, and that was
by the Saviour's taking our place, which He did; and now His
obedient followers share with Him this glory.

*In every time of testing, sorrow or suffering, may we look
to You, our eternal salvation, and find the promised comfort
and help. Amen.*

Source of eternal salvation - NIV

THE FORERUNNER

> Whither the forerunner is for us entered, even Jesus.
> *(Hebrews 6:20)*

"Our hope is fixed on nothing less than Jesus' blood and
righteousness." Our hope is an anchor which enters into that
which is beyond the veil, and our "Forerunner" has gone before us and entered beyond the veil into the Holy of Holies.
Our hope is anchored in Him. How safe it is! How satisfying it
is! We are a part of Him. We can never be separated from
Him because He lives in us and we shall live and be with Him
forever. Let our souls go out in unbounded thanksgiving.

*Lord Jesus, our great Forerunner, we rejoice in You today.
You are in the glory. We are looking forward to being with
You and like You. Come quickly and receive us unto Yourself.
Amen.*

Who went before us - NIV

KING OF RIGHTEOUSNESS

> First being by interpretation, King of righteousness.
> *(Hebrews 7:2)*

The picture is taken from the story of Melchisedec, the mysterious king to whom Abram paid tithes (Genesis 14). Christ is King of righteousness, for He is the King of kings. He is *the* Righteous One and the *only* Righteous One. We have no righteousness. All of our righteousness is as filthy rags, but "Christ is the end of the law for righteousness to everyone that believes." We believe in Him, and faith is counted unto us for righteousness. His righteousness is paid to our account, and we are associated with the Righteous King forever. Hallelujah!

Lord, we confess our unworthiness, but we rejoice in Your finished work and in the gift of Your righteousness to us. Let us rely only upon Your righteousness. Amen.

KING OF PEACE

> After that, also, King of Salem, which is, King of peace.
> *(Hebrews 7:2)*

Righteousness is the basis of peace. There is no peace for the wicked. "He is our peace, who hath made both one, and hath broken down the middle wall of partition between [Jew and Gentile] . . . to make in himself of twain one new man, so making peace." Remember what the King of Peace said, "Peace I leave with you, my peace I give unto you. . . . Let not your heart be troubled, neither let it be afraid." He dwells in us and we dwell in Him. He came and preached peace. He went to the cross and made peace possible. "Great peace have they which love Your law."

O King of Peace, may Your peace which passes all understanding garrison our souls this day. Break down the walls between us. Amen.

SURETY OF A BETTER TESTAMENT

By so much was Jesus made a surety of a better testament. *(Hebrews 7:22)*

Sometimes we lack assurance. We tremble, perhaps, and lack confidence in the finished work which our Christ has completed in us. But we have here the statement that Christ has become our Surety, or Security. He has placed Himself as our Bondsman. We can draw our drafts upon the Bank of Heaven, and He has pledged Himself as our Security. "Whatsoever you shall ask in My name, that will I do." Why have we so little faith in His pledged Word? Giving does not impoverish Him, nor withholding enrich Him. Let us honor Him by asking today, in His precious Name, large things for His glory.

Lord, with You as our Security we cannot fail. Amen.

The guarantee of a better covenant - NIV

OUR INTERCESSOR

Wherefore he is able also to save them to the uttermost that come unto God by him, seeing he ever liveth to make intercession for them. *(Hebrews 7:25)*

He saves to the fullest extent, for He ever lives and He ever represents us and meets all the charges against us. "And he saw that there was no man, and wondered that there was no intercessor: therefore his arm brought salvation unto him; and his righteousness, it sustained him" (Isaiah 59:16). The Holy Spirit also makes intercession for us with "groanings which cannot be uttered." Satan may bring charges against us, and sometimes they may be well founded, but He is there. He bore our sins, carried our sorrows, meets every accusation. What a wonderful Saviour and Intercessor!

Our Lord, we draw near in full assurance of faith. You will never leave us nor forsake us. We glorify Your name now and will ever throughout eternity. Amen.

SEPARATE FROM SINNERS

For such an high priest became us who is . . . separate from sinners. *(Hebrews 7:26)*

We use this as a title (or attribute) of our Lord because preachers and teachers are drifting so far from the belief in the divinity of Christ. But remember that the sin question could only be settled by a *sinless* Man—a *spotless* Lamb. Such was He who *knew* no sin though He *became* sin for us, that we might become the righteousness of God in Him. But, though He was separate from sinners He did not avoid them as we are inclined to do. No one ever loved them as He did— the Holy One. We must not miss this suggestion if we are to be like Him, loving sinners and following His example.

Lord Jesus, give us a genuine love for lost souls and a passion for their salvation. Help us to realize we are all sinners in need of You, the sinless One. Amen.

HIGHER THAN THE HEAVENS

For such an high priest became us, who is . . . higher than the heavens. *(Hebrews 7:26)*

This wonderful High Priest, the spotless Lamb of God, when He had finished His priestly sin-offering, sat down at the right hand of God. Yet we can see Him, the unchangeable Christ, with wounded hands and feet bearing testimony to His individuality and unchanging personality. Some day from the dizzy heights He will descend with a shout. His voice will ring out in glad expectancy. He is coming for you and for me. Wonder of wonders! Our faith in His finished work has sealed us forever to Him.

O Lord, You who are higher than the heavens, we give You all praise and wait with glad hearts for Your coming. Let us look up to the heavens where our help is found. Amen.

MINISTER OF THE SANCTUARY

A minister of the sanctuary, and of the true tabernacle, which the Lord pitched, and not man. *(Hebrews 8:2)*

We are carried back to the picture of the tabernacle and of the temple where God's High Priest officiated. He represented God in all of the ceremonies of the holy assembly. Here we have the promised Messiah, the Lord Jesus Christ, in the capacity of the Minister (or servant) of the Sanctuary. He is the King, but He is still a servant of men, serving in our behalf, loving us, ministering to us. Dwelling in our heart by the Holy Spirit, He performs every needed function in the cleansing and preparing of His people for their access to God.

We thank You, Lord Jesus, for Your marvelous ministry in our behalf. May we always seek access to the Father through You. Amen.

Serves in the sanctuary - NIV

MEDIATOR OF A BETTER COVENANT

But now . . . he is the mediator of a better covenant. *(Hebrews 8:6)*

Aaron was the high priest of the sanctuary of the old covenant, but now Christ in heaven is the "Mediator of a Better Covenant"—a Heavenly Covenant—God's agreement to confer blessings upon men. He promises to put His laws into their minds and write them on their hearts. He says, "I will be their God and they shall be my people . . . their sins and iniquities will I remember no more." Let us remember, then, that we are His sanctuary, His temple, and He will perfect His work in and through us. Acknowledge His will and let our temples be holy before the Lord.

Help us, great Mediator, to surrender all to You. Cleanse us, keep us cleansed that we may offer acceptable worship unto You. Amen.

THE TESTATOR

> For where a testament is, there must also of necessity be the death of the testator. *(Hebrews 9:16)*

A testator is a person who makes and leaves a will, or testament, at death. Christ has left a testament and a will. He died for us. He shed His blood as a free-will offering in our behalf. Under the law we were condemned to death. "The soul that sins, it shall die." "Death passed upon all men, for that all have sinned." The sin question is settled forever for us who believe in Jesus Christ, our "Testator." He died in our place. He ever lives. He represents us in the presence of the Father.

Lord, we lift our hearts to You and rejoice in the finished work and testimony of our Testator. You are the One who has sealed an everlasting covenant of mercy; we praise and thank You. Amen.

The one who made the will - NIV

HE THAT SHALL COME

> For yet a little while, and he that shall come will come, and will not tarry. *(Hebrews 10:37)*

The Christian life is built not only on the present but on the unseen future. Our life is a life of faith, a faith tried and tested and proven; fixed upon the unerring, unbreakable Word of God. God has never broken a promise and He never can. We can bank with unfailing confidence upon His written and living Word. Nothing pleases our Lord more than implicit faith in His Word and work. Nothing gives us such rest and joy as does this childlike faith. We must not be moved by the theories or doubts of men. When in doubt, read Hebrews 11.

Lord, we are looking for Your coming in the clouds of glory. Come quickly! In the meantime let us spend every one of our days preparing for You. Amen.

He who is coming - NIV

A REWARDER

But without faith it is impossible to please him: for he that cometh to God must believe that he is, and that he is a rewarder of them that diligently seek him. *(Hebrews 11:6)*

We come to God only through Jesus Christ. "No man cometh unto the Father but by me." And our Lord Jesus Christ is the judge: "For the Father judgeth no man, but hath committed all judgment unto the Son" (John 5:22). He pronounces the sentence. He gives the reward: "And, behold, I come quickly; and my reward is with me" (Revelation 22:12). We must do our work in His name and for His glory: "Knowing that of the Lord ye shall receive the reward of the inheritance: for ye serve the Lord Christ" (Colossians 3:24). We must live for Him and be willing to die for Him. Our reward awaits us.

Lord, we commit ourselves to You. Use us this day for Your glory. Whether we live or die, let us do it for You, Lord Jesus. Amen.

THE AUTHOR OF OUR FAITH

Looking unto Jesus the author . . . of our faith. *(Hebrews 12:2)*

The Author (Leader) of our faith is Jesus. Look to Him, for the inspiration to faith is found in Him. He is the prophesied and promised "Seed of the woman," bruised by Satan. He paid the penalty and then robbed the grave of its power, rose in the majesty of His glorified body and will come some day to bruise the serpent's head, conquer him, and imprison him. He inspires us by His sacrificial death and by His precious promises. His message is, "Follow Me. I will never leave you nor forsake you." And our response to Him should be, "Lead on; we will follow You even unto death."

O great Author of Our Faith, may we keep our eyes on You and with unwavering faith follow You to the end. We pray You will complete this great work on our behalf. Amen.

THE FINISHER OF OUR FAITH

Looking unto Jesus the . . . finisher of our faith. *(Hebrews 12:2)*

He is the captain, and He leads His hosts with the Sword of the Spirit in His hand. And He is the Finisher (Completer) of our faith. Our Lord set us the example of faith and He will perfect it in us. We see Jesus who for the joy that was set before Him endured the cross and has now sat down at the right hand of God. He *finished* His work of faith, and by grace He will finish it in our experience. There will be trials, there will be severe testings, but we are to "count it all joy." He finished, and day by day and step by step, He leads us on. The best is always before us, though the last link may be the cross—but then, we will be "face to face with Him!"

Lord, hold us fast by the power of faith until we finish our course, and let us run that course with great joy. Amen.

The perfecter of our faith - NIV

MEDIATOR OF THE NEW COVENANT

And to Jesus the mediator of the new covenant, and to the blood of sprinkling, that speaketh better things than that of Abel. *(Hebrews 12:24)*

The Christian life is a strange life, a journey through wilderness experiences, but we always have something better before us. The door posts are sprinkled with blood. We are safe. Old things have passed away. The blood of Jesus Christ, God's Son, cleanses us from *all* sin. The blood speaks of His sacrificial, finished work. Let us rest under the cross. Let us see the blood. Let it separate us from a sinful world and make of us witnesses to its cleansing power.

Lord, give us the needed grace to witness today and every day to the efficacy of the atoning blood of the New Covenant. It is blood sufficient for everything we face in this life. Amen.

MY HELPER

> So that we may boldly say, the Lord is my helper. *(Hebrews 13:6)*

What a difference there is in believers! How timid some are. Is it because they do not know the promises? "The fear of man bringeth a snare: but whoso putteth his trust in the Lord shall be safe." "The angel of the Lord encampeth round about them that fear him, and delivereth them." Courage of conviction is the crying need of the Christian today—conviction based on God's Holy Word and God's call to service. He has said, "I will never leave you nor forsake you." Faith takes hold upon this promise and allows nothing to move it.

Lord Jesus, our Helper, help us to lean hard upon Your gracious promises and have a joyful life today. Let us be bold and courageous, knowing that You are our Helper in everything. Amen.

THE GREAT SHEPHERD OF THE SHEEP

> Our Lord Jesus, that great shepherd of the sheep. *(Hebrews 13:20)*

In the sixth chapter of Mark we have a touching picture of our Lord Jesus. He had been apart with His disciples in a desert place and, when He "saw much people, [He] was moved with compassion toward them, because they were as sheep not having a shepherd: and he began to teach them many things." He was the promised Shepherd. He is here pictured as the Great Shepherd, raised from the dead, sanctified by the blood of the everlasting covenant, which is able to make us "perfect in every good work to do his will" (Hebrews 13:21). How? By working in us and through us that which pleases Himself.

Lord, we are Your sheep. Take us, mold us, and make of us that which shall please You, and we will give You all the glory. Amen.

THAT WORTHY NAME

> Do not they blaspheme that worthy name by which ye are
> called? *(James 2:7)*

James urges the saints not to have partiality in their attitude
toward men who have wealth or position. The emphasis is on
Christ's "Worthy Name." That Name is sacred; "there is none
other name . . . whereby we must be saved." God has "given
him a name which is above every name: that at the name of
Jesus every knee should bow," though for those who are
compelled to bow, it will be too late. In that Name we approach our Father; in that Name we have our title to heaven.

*Lord Jesus, we come in Your Worthy Name and ask for
forgiveness for our sins of neglect and ask for Your power for
service this day. You are worthy of a standard of excellence
in all we do. Amen.*

The noble name - NIV

A LAMB WITHOUT BLEMISH OR SPOT

> But with the precious blood of Christ, as of a lamb without
> blemish and without spot. *(1 Peter 1:19)*

Familiarity with scriptural terms often causes us to minimize
their meaning. Here we have two words so wonderful that we
are hesitant in our effort to make any comment—"Blood" and
"Lamb." How precious the Blood! Millions of drops were
poured out through the ages from Abel to Christ and every
drop said: "The Lamb is not yet. But He will come. We are the
testimony of His coming." And finally the Pure Lamb of God
finished the work of redemption. Is He so precious to us that
we would be willing to die in His behalf? If so, let us tell Him,

*"O Lamb of God, my Saviour, purchased by Your precious
blood, I surrender all to You now. Thank You for your perfect
work of redemption." Amen.*

A lamb without blemish or defect - NIV

A LIVING STONE

To whom coming, as unto a living stone, disallowed indeed of men, but chosen of God, and precious. *(1 Peter 2:4)*

Words are inadequate to describe the mysteries of heaven. It is not composed of an inert mass like the stones of earth, but of *living, life-imparting* stones. He is living. He will always be living. He lives in the lives of the redeemed. He is the chosen of God. He is the Stone cut out of the mountain which is to crush the nations. He is the One in whom and through whom we have everlasting life. He lives and will live throughout eternity, and we will live in and with Him. Hallelujah!

Dear Lord, our Rock, our Foundation Stone, we rest in the security of Your eternal life. Manifest that life through us today. Amen.

A CHIEF CORNER STONE

Behold, I lay in Sion a chief corner stone . . . and he that believeth on him shall not be confounded. *(1 Peter 2:6)*

Every structure must have a foundation, and those of special honor must have a cornerstone. Christ is the "Chief Corner Stone" of the most wonderful temple ever conceived. This temple is built of human lives—blood-washed saints of the Living God. It is the dwelling place of God the Father, God the Son, and God the Holy Spirit. Over the door are inscribed the words, "Holiness unto the Lord." From the dome the chimes ring out the call,"Exalt the Lord our God and worship at His feet."

O Lord, may we be the mouthpieces to spread the invitation to others to come to the temple for worship. May all the earth worship Your majesty and give You praise. Amen.

A chosen and precious cornerstone - NIV

A STONE OF STUMBLING

The stone which the builders disallowed . . . is made . . . a Stone of Stumbling. *(1 Peter 2:7–8)*

A corner stone upon which the whole world was built, upon which the church is built, and a "Stone of Stumbling!" How can that be? To those who willfully reject Him, as did the Jewish nation, and stumble into the abyss, there is weeping and wailing and gnashing of teeth. To those who pride themselves on their education, wealth, or position, and refuse to bow at His feet, He is a Stone of Stumbling. How subtle is Satan! How hard is the human heart! How our hearts ache for those who know Him not.

Lord, You are precious to us. Help us to remove the stumbling block by living out a life that shall win some souls to You. Amen.

A stone that causes men to stumble - NIV

A ROCK OF OFFENCE

The stone which the builders disallowed . . . is made . . . a rock of offence. *(1 Peter 2:7–8)*

Many of the Jewish people rejected Christ even though He displayed the works and words of God. Every possible effort was made by Christ to win His own people to Himself. But they would not have Him. Without the grace of God we would all reject our Savior, but He has called us by His mercy through the finished work of Christ. How can it be that our loving, crucified Lord should become to so many a "Rock of Offense" instead of the "Chief Corner Stone"?

O Lord, keep our feet on the Rock and our hearts loving You. May our lives be holy, not an offense to You or our neighbors. Amen.

A rock that makes men fall - NIV

THE BISHOP OF SOULS

> For ye were as sheep going astray; but are now returned unto the Shepherd and Bishop of your souls. *(1 Peter 2:25)*

The elders of the early church were "overseers"—called to care for the flock as under-shepherds. Here Christ is set before us as the One who directs the under-shepherds. He is "the Bishop of our souls." He imparts life which is eternal, which He purchased for us by His own sacrifice. His eye is upon us. His heart goes out in love to the lost, straying sheep and He never fails in His own good way and time to bring them back to the fold (the church). God will judge those who selfishly seek and faithlessly serve as under-shepherds. "Seek you great things for yourself? Seek them not."

Lord, help us to recognize You as our Bishop and to be subject to Your guidance. Hold us. Keep us under Your care, as we would extend that care to others. Amen.

Overseer of your souls - NIV

THE CHIEF SHEPHERD

> And when the chief Shepherd shall appear, ye shall receive a crown of glory that fadeth not away. *(1 Peter 5:4)*

Christ as our shepherd has already been considered as "the door of the sheep," "the good shepherd," "the one shepherd," "the great shepherd," and now we have the climax in "The Chief Shepherd." In Him is vested all authority and power. He will give the rewards to the faithful. We will share His glory. We visualize Him with shepherd staff leading, guiding, directing His sheep, enfolding them in safety. But on the glad day which is to come He will crown His loyal ones. Is anything more to be desired than the privilege accorded us of making Him now the chiefest of ten thousand in our hearts?

Lord, be You to us today the loving and caring Shepherd that we have known from Your Word. Amen.

THE DAY STAR

> We have also a more sure word of prophecy; whereunto ye do well that ye take heed . . . until . . . the day star arise in your hearts. *(2 Peter 1:19)*

In the gospel of John, we read: "In him was life; and the life was the light of men." We have the sure Word of God. It is a lamp to our feet and a light to our path. Our hearts are darkened by the evil nature within us, but when Jesus comes into our hearts He illumines the Word of God and shines with all the effulgence of His glory. Perpetual day is for those who walk in His light. Every day is a good day and the eternal glory awaits us.

Blessed Lord, our Light, shine in our hearts and lives this day. May we reflect Your glory. Amen.

The morning star - NIV

THE WORD OF LIFE

> That which . . . our hands have handled, of the Word of life. *(1 John 1:1)*

John 1:1 says: "In the beginning was the Word, and the Word was with God, and the Word was God. The same was in the beginning with God," and this truth bewilders us; but here we have John saying concerning Him who was God that he had looked upon Him and handled Him. He, Himself, said to doubting Thomas, "Handle Me and see. A spirit has not flesh and bones as you see I have." He is the Life-giving Word. The need of a lost world is to know Him. The business of believers is to tell the wonderful story. Paint the picture. Live the life. Sow the seed. And you will find Him growing into your own life.

God the Word, how we thank You for the revelation of Yourself to us. We are Yours. You are ours. Amen.

THAT ETERNAL LIFE

> That eternal life, which was with the Father, and was manifested unto us. *(1 John 1:2)*

John says, "We have seen Him who is Life Eternal. We are witnesses to that fact, and we want you to have the assurance that your joy may be full." And Paul says, "For in Him dwells all the fullness of the Godhead bodily." *He is* "Eternal Life." He has imparted Eternal Life to us through the channel of faith, and the indwelling Holy Spirit testifies to it. Nothing can ever separate us from the love of God which is in Christ Jesus our Lord. We are God's rich sons. Our treasures are for evermore. "Oh, happy day, that fixed our choice!" Let us go out and tell it anywhere and everywhere.

O Blessed One, our Eternal Life, we wait for Your coming. Come quickly. Fill us with Your Spirit and Word of Life. Amen.

THE ADVOCATE

> My little children, these things write I unto you, that ye sin not. And if any man sin, we have an advocate with the Father, Jesus Christ the righteous. *(1 John 2:1)*

Sin is the existing nature of man. God, in love, has recognized the need of man and has made provision for that need. We sin when we "come short of the glory of God." So Christ becomes our "Advocate" or "One who comes alongside," which is the meaning of "advocate." He comes to stand by us. When Satan charges us with sin, Christ represents us and defends us. He is the Attorney who handles our case. His propitiation (or covering for sin) is manifested in all His work for us—in His life, His death, His resurrection, His ascension, and His intercession.

Lord, we thank You that You appear for us and that through You, we are all adopted by our heavenly Father. Let us live as true members of your family. Amen.

JESUS CHRIST THE RIGHTEOUS

If any man sin, we have an advocate with the Father, Jesus Christ the righteous. *(1 John 2:1)*

Jesus Christ is the "Righteous One." "Righteous" means "right" or "just." There never was another perfectly righteous man, for the Scripture says, "There is none righteous; *no not one.*" "All have sinned." No unrighteous man could be our Advocate or Judge. He must Himself be just, and He is also the Justifier (Romans 3:20). What a consolation to us as poor sinners to know that we are justified from all things from which we could not be justified by the Law of Moses.

Lord Jesus, we pour out our hearts to You. You have settled forever what we could never have settled. We are judged righteous and innocent. Hallelujah! Amen.

THE SAVIOUR OF THE WORLD

And we have seen and do testify that the Father sent the Son to be the Saviour of the world. *(1 John 4:14)*

A lost and ruined world, bound by the shackles of sin, dominated by the demon Satan, helpless and hopeless! What can be done? Only God, the Sovereign against whom the world has sinned, can solve the question, and He has. He sent His Son. We have seen Him by faith and testify to the truth that He is indeed a Saviour. He has saved us through faith in His name and finished work. We *must* testify. We *must* bear witness. Wherever we go, whatever we do, let us tell it to all—"He is the world Saviour."

Lord, may we be faithful witnesses to Your saving power and tell the love story to all. There is only one Sovereign and Redeemer—Jesus Christ our Saviour. Amen.

THE TRUE GOD

> And we know that the Son of God is come, and hath given us
> an understanding, that we may know him that is true; and we
> are in him that is true, even in his Son Jesus Christ. This is the
> true God, and eternal life. *(1 John 5:20)*

In His prayer on that last night, Jesus said to the Father: "This
is life eternal that they should know You, the only true God,
and Jesus Christ whom You have sent." Here it is evident that
"we are in him that is true, even his Son Jesus Christ, the *True
God* and eternal life." There is but *one* God. "Great is the
mystery of godliness." We praise God—*the True God*—that
we are in Him and He in us. Nothing can ever separate us.

*Lord Jesus, You who are the True God, help us to live that
great and glorious life that You have imparted to us. Amen.*

THE SON OF THE FATHER

> Grace be with you, mercy, and peace, from God the Father,
> and from the Lord Jesus Christ, the Son of the Father, in truth
> and love. *(2 John 3)*

Here is a threefold blessing bestowed by John: "Grace, mercy, and peace from the Son of the Father." This is the testimony of the Father: "This is my beloved Son in whom I am well
pleased" and He is the *only begotten* of the Father. There is
no separation between Father and Son. The union is unbreakable. "He that has seen me has seen the Father." "I and My
Father are one." The blessing is to be bestowed in "truth and
love." Truth without love may be cold, hard, harsh. Love without truth may be purely sentimental, but, when combined,
they truly represent the message of "the Son of the Father,"
for the Son *is* the Truth, revealed in Love.

*We pray, our Father, that this benediction of grace, mercy,
and peace may rest upon us this day as we meditate upon
the Son of the Father. Amen.*

THE FAITHFUL WITNESS

Jesus Christ, who is the faithful witness. *(Revelation 1:5)*

This was the testimony of Christ Himself when He stood before Pilate (John 18:37): "To this end was I born, and for this cause came I into the world, that I should bear witness unto the truth. Every one that is of the truth heareth my voice." This was His mission—to bear faithful witness. This is the obligation of every believer, "You shall be witnesses of me." This is the failure in a large measure of the church. The unsaved are waiting for the testimony by lip and life of professing Christians, and as they behold it, they are convicted by the Holy Spirit.

May the Holy Spirit Himself so control our lives that we shall count it our highest privilege to witness of Him before a skeptical world. Amen.

THE FIRST BEGOTTEN OF THE DEAD

Jesus Christ, who is . . . the first begotten of the dead. *(Revelation 1:5)*

Jesus Christ raised Lazarus from the dead, but He Himself came forth from the grave by His own power. Lazarus died again, but Jesus Christ "ever lives to make intercession for us." He was "The Firstborn from the Dead." He is the forerunner of the saints who shall also be raised from the dead. "But now is Christ risen from the dead, and become the firstfruits of them that slept." "We know that, when he shall appear, we shall be like him; for we shall see him as he is." "Who shall change our vile body, that it may be fashioned like unto his glorious body."

Our Lord, we look and long for Your coming in Your glorified body that we may be with You and like You. We long also to be risen from the dead with You in glory. Amen.

The firstborn from the dead - NIV

THE PRINCE OF THE KINGS OF THE EARTH

Jesus Christ, who is . . . the prince of the kings of the earth. *(Revelation 1:5)*

A glorious title! Sometime in the future there will be a gathering of all the hosts that have ever lived on this earth, and of the hosts of heaven, and in their presence will stand *One* who will be proclaimed "Prince of the kings of the earth—King of kings and Lord of lords!" The kingdoms of the world are His by right and title, and before Him all must bow. He is Lord of all who exercise authority and King of all who reign. He has not yet asserted His authoritative rights. They are still in reserve, but the day is coming when every scepter will be broken and every crown laid at His feet.

We praise You, Lord of Hosts, our Saviour; we will be with You then. Help us to do our best to hasten the glad day. May Your grace and power work in us to the end. Amen.

The ruler of the kings of the earth - NIV

ALPHA AND OMEGA

I am Alpha and Omega, the beginning and the ending, saith the Lord, which is, and which was, and which is to come, the Almighty. *(Revelation 1:8)*

"Alpha" is the first letter of the Greek alphabet, and "Omega" is the last. So our Lord is First and Last. He is the Source of all things. He is the Source of all truth, of all the promises given in the Word of God, of all the prophecies, of all commands and of all penalties. How great is our Lord, "which is and which was and which is to come"—the All-inclusive One! Everything is involved in the two words, "beginning" and "ending," and one word includes it all—"IS."

O Jehovah-Elohim, First and Last, who sees and knows all things, hold us in Your hand. Amen.

THE ALMIGHTY

I am . . . the Almighty. *(Revelation 1:8)*

Our Lord Jesus Christ is the All-sufficient One. Listen to His voice—the "I AM" speaking to us. His voice and message demand attention and obedience. We can trust Him and trust His message. Nothing can fail of all that He says. The Bible is an infallible Book. Its message is an infallible message and it says: "I will receive you, and will be a Father unto you, and ye shall be my sons and daughters, saith the Lord Almighty" (2 Corinthians 6:17–18). And again, "He that dwelleth in the secret place of the Most High shall abide under the shadow of the Almighty" (Psalm 91:1). What an abiding place for us who are His dear children!

Almighty One, we submit to You today, and to Your all-encompassing power. Help us to dwell with and in You. Amen.

THE FIRST AND THE LAST

And he laid his right hand upon me, saying unto me, Fear not; I am the first and the last. *(Revelation 1:17)*

He was the First begotten. He said of Himself, "Before Abraham was, I am." And John the Baptist said, "He was before me." "In the beginning was the Word, and the Word was with God, and the Word was God. The same was in the beginning with God." He puts His right hand on us, that hand of power, and says in tenderest tones, "Fear not." He draws us to Himself with that same hand and says, "Pillow your head upon My shoulder. Have no fear. You are Mine. I purchased you at a great price. Perfect love casts out fear." He was *First* in His love for us when we were in sin. He is the *Last One* to forget or forsake us.

Blessed Lord, may we have that perfect love which casts out all fear, seeing You at the beginning and end of all our days. Amen.

HE THAT LIVES

I am he that liveth, and was dead; and behold, I am alive for evermore, Amen. *(Revelation 1:18)*

He lives and abides forever. He ever lives to make intercession for us. In love for us and through grace He died for us. He bowed His head and gave up His Spirit. The bars of death were broken. He tore them away. He is living now and will live throughout ages, and He holds the keys of death and hell. "He has the keys"—the complete mastery. He has the right to open and shut. Binding and loosing are at His command. The sting of death is sin and the strength of sin is the law, but thanks be to God who gives us the victory through our Lord Jesus Christ! Praise be to Your name, Victor over death!

We await Your coming and the shout from heaven. May Your keys keep out all evil from our lives. Renew us in Your image. Amen.

The Living One - NIV

THE MORNING STAR

And I will give him the morning star. *(Revelation 2:28)*

He will give us Himself, for He is "The Morning Star." Again, we hear the voice of the Holy Spirit coming with a heart message for the beloved of the Lord. We are bone of His bone and flesh of His flesh. The stars are for the night, and it is night now for this poor broken world that lies in the lap of the Wicked One. It grows darker and darker and midnight is upon us, but our eyes are heavenward. We hear His promise. As the Sun of Righteousness to Israel He brought them blessings; but before the glad day for the church comes, the Morning Star must shine, and a ray of light will appear for His own heavenly ones.

Lord, keep us close to You. Keep us loyal. Keep our eyes upon the skies as we labor for You and Your coming. Amen.

THE HIDDEN MANNA

> To him that overcometh will I give to eat of the hidden manna. *(Revelation 2:17)*

What is this "Hidden Manna"? Is it not Him who is the Bread of Life? The voice of the Holy Spirit is heard speaking to the churches a message for the overcomers. Food awaits them. For twelve thousand and five hundred days manna was rained down from heaven for the children of Israel. From the glory land our Lord feeds His flock with the Word of God—the Word made flesh. We who feed upon Him shall live forever. We have the white stone and the new name.

You are speaking to us, our Lord. We hear. We await the day and the new name which You will give to us. Even now, let us eat of the bread of life, our eternal food. Amen.

THE AMEN

> These things saith the Amen. *(Revelation 3:14)*

"Amen" is "So be it," or "So it is." The "Amen" here is our Lord—the Faithful Witness. He has said "Amen" to every truth of the Scripture, but the church has failed to follow in His footsteps. She has the truth for she has Himself, and He is the Way, the Truth, and the Life, as we have seen; but she has not said "Amen." She says, "I am rich and increased with goods and have need of nothing." She has not been a faithful and true witness. She has been neither cold nor hot, but a lukewarm product. To what extent are we responsible? God forgive us and help us! Yet we know that Christ will perfect His church.

Lord, open our eyes to see, our ears to hear, and our hearts to believe. Baptize us with the power of the Holy Spirit. You are the last word in all things. Amen.

THE FAITHFUL AND TRUE WITNESS

> These things saith . . . the faithful and true witness.
> *(Revelation 3:14)*

We have viewed Him as the Faithful Witness, but He is also the Faithful and *True* Witness. How marvelously the Holy Spirit emphasizes the character of Christ for us. Here we have the "Amen" amplified. The word "Faithful" asserts the truthfulness of "True" for it implies "real and complete." He had seen that which He attested, and He was competent and willing to witness. Has the church been a faithful and true witness? No, she has not. Let us come a little closer. Have *we* been faithful and true witnesses? Alas, we must bow our heads with regret as we recognize our failure. Yet God works through us and will continue in greater measure by His grace.

O Lord our Saviour, forgive us for our faithlessness as witnesses. Anoint us to stand before a lost world and be true at any cost. Amen.

THE BEGINNING OF THE CREATION OF GOD

> These things saith . . . the beginning of the creation of God.
> *(Revelation 3:14)*

Four headships are ascribed to our Lord Jesus Christ. First—of the body: "Head over all things to the church, which is his body" (Ephesians 1:22–23). Second—of the race: "Ye are all one in Christ Jesus" (Galatians 3:28). Third—of the creation: "Who is the image of the invisible God, the firstborn of every creature" (Colossians 1:15). Fourth—of every man: "But I would have you know, that the head of every man is Christ" (1 Corinthians 11:3).

O Mighty One, Creator of all things, help us to love and serve You. Complete the work You have begun in us as part of Your larger magnificent work. Amen.

The ruler of God's creation - NIV

THE LION OF THE TRIBE OF JUDAH

> Behold, the Lion of the tribe of Judah . . . hath prevailed to open the book and to loose the seals thereof. *(Revelation 5:5)*

Jacob's dying prophecy was fulfilled in Jesus: "The sceptre shall not depart from Judah, nor a law-giver from between his feet until Shiloh come." (Genesis 49:10). Judah had no conception that nearly three thousand years would pass before his prophecy would or could be fulfilled, or that its fulfillment would involve the glorified Son of God. The characteristics of a lion are manifest in the life and work of the Messiah. He will arrest every opposing force of Satan and establish His universal kingdom. Glory be to God, we will be with Him and be like Him in the final overthrow of Satan's kingdom.

Lord, help us to be like You now. Help us to wear the armor of warriors and carry the Sword of the Spirit, being as bold as lions on Your behalf. Amen.

THE ROOT OF DAVID

> Weep not; behold the Lion of the tribe of Judah, the Root of David, hath prevailed. *(Revelation 5:5)*

King David was the representative of *Royalty;* Moses of the *Law;* Abraham of the *Promises.* Here, Christ is seen in relation to His throne and kingdom rights. "A Root" from the stem, or branch, of David: "And there shall come forth a rod out of the stem of Jesse, and a Branch shall grow out of his roots" (Isaiah 11:1). Jesus was the Root that was to rise and reign over the Gentiles and in Him would the Gentiles trust. What wonders confront us concerning Him! His very life can take root within us to bear the fruit of righteousness.

Lord, we marvel more and more that You could ever love us and die for us, You who are the Mighty One. But we bow at Your feet in worship and praise. Amen.

HOLY AND TRUE

> How long, O Lord, holy and true, dost thou not judge and
> avenge our blood on them that dwell on the earth?
> *(Revelation 6:10)*

This is the heart cry of those who suffered death for Jesus'
sake because they were true to Him in life and testimony. Is it
not such a cry as sometimes bursts forth from our own souls
as we see the hellish hatred of Satan for the souls of men?
"How long, O Lord, how long, You Holy and True One?" But
we must abide in faith. He says, "What I do you know not
now but you shall know hereafter." How marvelous is the
grace and patience of God our Saviour! But the day is coming
when the Righteous Judge will render His judgment.

*O Holy and True One, we look to You in full assurance of
faith. Keep us close to Yourself this day. May You say, "Well
done good and faithful servant" on the great judgment day.
Amen.*

THE LAMB IN THE MIDST OF THE THRONE

> For the Lamb which is in the midst of the throne shall feed
> them, and shall lead them unto living fountains of waters: and
> God shall wipe away all tears from their eyes. *(Revelation 7:17)*

Here is a wonderful picture of our future dwelling place. We
are before the throne of God. Our robes have been made
white in the blood of the Lamb. We shall not know hunger or
thirst anymore. He that sits upon the throne shall feed us, and
we shall drink from the living fountains. Tears will be wiped
away forever. What has made all this possible? *One Thing*—
the blood! *One Person*—the Lamb! We shall dwell through
eternity with Him, be with Him, and be like Him.

*Wonderful Lord and wonderful Love, help us to dwell ever
in Your presence. Feed us with heavenly manna now. Amen.*
The Lamb at the center of the throne - NIV

THE LAMB SLAIN

> And all that dwell upon the earth shall worship him, whose names are not written in the book of life of the Lamb slain from the foundation of the world. *(Revelation 13:8)*

Jesus was ordained from the foundation of the world to suffer upon the cross for our sins. The death of Christ has been effective in paying the penalty for sin, from the beginning. The only means of salvation for men has been the shedding of His blood. That was foreknown and foreordained of God. What a place in our hearts should the Lamb of God have! What a place should the blood of Christ have, by which we are redeemed! For "without the shedding of blood there is no remission."

Blessed Lamb of God, we adore You. We rejoice that we are washed in Your blood. You will be known throughout eternity as the Lamb that was slain. Amen.

KING OF SAINTS

> Just and true are thy ways, thou King of saints. *(Revelation 15:3)*

This title is better rendered "King of Nations" or "King of the Ages." What a picture is here! We are standing by the glassy sea, mingled with fire. A judgment is awaiting the nations. Seven angels with seven last plagues are there. Mark seems to describe this time: "For in those days shall be affliction, such as was not from the beginning of the creation which God created unto this time, neither shall be" (Mark 13:19). But there are the harps of God and the song of Moses. The song is of victory over the beast and his image. What a day! What a joy for our adored Lord!

We pledge to You today our loyal devotion, King of Nations. Help us to do Your will until the coming of "the day." Show mercy to Your subjects who willingly serve You. Amen.
King of the ages - NIV

165

LORD OF LORDS

> For he is Lord of lords, and King of kings: and they that are with him are called, and chosen, and faithful. *(Revelation 17:14)*

From the Garden of Eden until the scene described in this verse, the powers of earth and hell have fought against our Lord. The prince of this world and the prince of the power of the air has shown his satanic hatred for Christ, the Promised One who will bruise his head. The world has been the sphere of the conflict of the ages, but, thanks be to God, the day when that war will cease is portrayed in this verse. All kings must bow to Him. It has been an age-long conflict, but the end must come. We look forward to the prophesied victory.

You who hold the worlds in the palm of Your hand, hasten the glad, victorious day of Your coming. Prepare us for conflict with the world as we seek to extend Your kingship in all areas. Amen.

KING OF KINGS

> The Lamb shall overcome them; for He is . . . King of kings. *(Revelation 17:14)*

He has upon His garments and upon His thigh the name "King of kings." Who has? The One who was born in a manger and who fellowshiped with fishermen as He longs to fellowship with us today. A sharp sword issues from His mouth —the Sword of the Spirit, which is the Word of God. As His enemies fell before His presence in the Garden, so they will always fall. The power of God's Word is *irresistible.* How foolish are they whose feeble hands are raised up against the King of kings—the Mighty One! What judgment awaits all those who oppose Him and His unerring Word.

King of kings, we bow to You. We follow You. Help us to fight the good fight of faith. Amen.

LORD GOD OMNIPOTENT

> And I heard as it were the voice of a great multitude, and as the voice of many waters, and as the voice of mighty thunderings, saying, Alleluia; for the Lord God omnipotent reigneth. *(Revelation 19:6)*

Here is a climax. What words can compare with the words of God associated with this matchless scene: "And after these things I heard a great voice of much people in Heaven, saying Alleluia; Salvation, and glory, and honor and power, unto the Lord our God . . . Let us be glad and rejoice and give honor to Him; for the marriage of the Lamb is come and His wife has made herself ready." The time is not far distant. The Omnipotent One is coming—and we will be with Him. Hallelujah!

You who are the Mighty One, gird us with Your strength, that we may do our best to hasten that glad day. Amen.

Lord God Almighty - NIV

WORD OF GOD

> And he was clothed with a vesture dipped in blood: and his name is called The Word of God. *(Revelation 19:13)*

How can we attempt to embody in a few words what this title demands? Only John uses the term. John says, "without him was not anything made that was made. . . . And the Word was made flesh." How glad we are that we have heard His Word. We have seen Him by faith. He dwells in us and among us. Clothed in blood-dipped garments, He leads the armies of heaven, including all the saints of the Old and New Testament, to victory. Pity those whose eyes have been closed to the vision of the real Christ and who only have a sentimental conception of Him.

We bow at Your feet, blessed Word of God, and lift our voices as we sing, "Hallelujah! What a Saviour!" Rule on the throne of our hearts now and forever. Amen.

THE TEMPLE

> And I saw no temple therein: for the Lord God Almighty and the Lamb are the temple of it. *(Revelation 21:22)*

What a wonderful temple! The Lord Himself is the Temple! The city is four-square, as was the Holy of Holies; twelve thousand furlongs—fifteen hundred square miles! Whatever significance there may be in the dimensions and the structure—whether literal or pictorial—it means, "Great in size; rich in adornment." The city is of pure gold, like clear glass; walls of jasper, upon that sapphire, then chalcedony, emerald, sardonyx, sardius, beryl, topaz, chrysoprasus, jacinth, amethyst; gates of one pearl each; streets of gold. We stand in awe, but—glory be to God—we anticipate with increasing joy the vision which awaits us and its full realization.

Blessed One, keep us close to You with open ears and open eyes, as we await the realization of our fond anticipation. We cannot comprehend the beauty of Your dwelling place. Amen.

THE LIGHT OF THE CITY

> And the Lamb is the light thereof. *(Revelation 21:23)*

The Lamb is the "Light of the World," and He is also the Light of the eternal, heavenly city. There is no need of sun or moon, for He who created all things has provided a Light for the City, and it is the glory of His own countenance—the Lamb of God who died upon the cross; the One who bore our sins and washed us in His own blood. By this Light the nations shall walk, and in this Light kings and people will pay their tribute. We will be there. Hallelujah!

Lamb of God, Light of the World, we bask in the sunshine of Your love now and will in the light of Your glory hereafter. Let us pay tribute now and in the New Jerusalem. Amen.

The lamp - NIV

THE OFFSPRING OF DAVID

I am the root and the offspring of David, and the bright and morning star. *(Revelation 22:16)*

Christ is the stem which sprang from the root of Jesse, and He is "The Offspring of David " God, the Son, created the heavens and the earth and all that are therein, yet He is the Offspring of David, David's Lord and David's Son. He was *born* King of the Jews and *died* King of the Jews and some day he will *reign* King of the Jews. This was God's promise and all of God's promises shall be fulfilled. As the Divine Creator, He is the Root of David's house; as man, He is the Offspring. There is no contradiction in God's Word concerning God's Son.

We glorify Your Word and Your work, our Lord. We look into Your face and adore You. You are the King of kings and Lord of lords as well as the son of David from Nazareth. Amen.

THE BRIGHT AND MORNING STAR

I Jesus have sent mine angel to testify unto you these things in the churches. I am . . . the bright and morning star. *(Revelation 22:16)*

We have meditated upon Christ as the "day star" and the "morning star," but here He, who is the light of the world, speaks of Himself as the "Bright and Morning Star." Before the rising of the sun, before the millennium dawns, He will be to the church the "Bright and Morning Star." He will dispel the darkness for us before the prophesied judgments come upon a weary, sin-sick world; and before the glories depicted in this chapter are revealed, He will appear as the Bright and Morning Star.

Lord, we are looking for the effulgent glory of Your presence, Bright and Morning Star. Dawn in our hearts, we pray, as a sign of the new dawn of Your eternal kingdom. Amen.

THE TESTIFIER

> He which testifieth these things saith, Surely I come quickly.
> Amen. Even so, come, Lord Jesus. *(Revelation 22:20)*

This is not a title, nor a name, but a fitting truth with which to close this little volume. We would rejoice if every reader had a heart-felt desire to say "Amen" to this promise of our Lord. The days grow darker for the church and for the world. The signs multiply as we look carefully at the prophecies. The poor decaying world reels like a drunken man to its doom. Our hearts are sad. We are thinking of those whose future is to be full of woe and anguish. Yet God continues to call sinners to Himself. "The Testifier" entreats us to go and testify to the lost. Let us point them to the Lamb of God and plead with sinners to accept Him and with the saints to look for Him. He has left *the Testimony* of His Word, with its precious promises. And now, in closing, the last verse of this chapter is our heartfelt prayer for our readers,

"The grace of our Lord Jesus Christ be with you all." Amen.

INDEX

Advocate, The (1 John 2:1), 154
All and in All (Colossians 3:11), 129
Almighty, The (Revelation 1:8), 159
Alpha and Omega (Revelation 1:8), 158
Altogether Lovely (Song of Solomon 5:16), 28
Amen, The (Revelation 3:14), 161
Ancient of Days (Daniel 7:13–14), 58
Angel of His Presence, The (Isaiah 63:9), 53
Angel of the Lord, The (Genesis 22:15), 11
Apostle, The (Hebrews 3:1), 138
Author of Eternal Salvation (Hebrews 5:9), 140
Author of Our Faith, The (Hebrews 12:2), 146

Babe, The (Luke 2:12), 80
Balm of Gilead (Jeremiah 8:22), 54
Beginning, The (Colossians 1:18), 127
Beginning of the Creation of God, The (Revelation 3:14), 162
Beloved, God's (Matthew 12:18), 68
Beloved Son, God's (Matthew 17:5), 70
Bishop of Souls, The (1 Peter 2:25), 152
Blessed and Only Potentate (1 Timothy 6:15), 132
Blessed Hope (Titus 2:13), 133
Branch of the Lord, The (Isaiah 4:2), 29

Branch out of Jesse's Roots, A (Isaiah 11:1), 35
Bread of Life, The (John 6:35), 94
Bridegroom, The (Matthew 25:10), 71
Bright and Morning Star, The (Revelation 22:16), 169
Brightness of His Glory, The (Hebrews 1:3), 135
Brother, Our (Mark 3:35), 72
Builder, The (Hebrews 3:3), 138
Bundle of Myrrh (Song of Solomon 1:13), 25

Captain of Our Salvation, The (Hebrews 2:10), 137
Captain of the Host of the Lord, The (Joshua 5:14), 14
Carpenter, The (Mark 6:3), 73
Chief Corner Stone, A (1 Peter 2:6), 150
Chief Shepherd, The (1 Peter 5:4), 152
Chiefest Among Ten Thousand, The (Song of Solomon 5:10), 28
Child, The (Isaiah 7:16), 30
Child Jesus, The (Luke 2:43), 83
Chosen of God, The (Luke 23:35), 87
Christ (Ephesians 1:3), 119
Christ of God, The (Luke 9:20), 85
Christ Our Life (Colossians 3:4), 128
Christ the Lord (Luke 2:11), 80
Christ, the Saviour of the World, The (John 4:42), 94
Christ, the Son of the Blessed (Mark 14:61), 76
Cluster of Camphire (Song of Solomon 1:14), 26
Commander, A (Isaiah 55:4), 52
Consolation of Israel, The (Luke 2:25), 81
Counsellor (Isaiah 9:6), 32

Creator of All Things (Colossians 1:16), 126
Crown of Glory, A (Isaiah 28:5), 40

Day Star, The (2 Peter 1:19), 153
Daysman, The (Job 9:33), 16
Dayspring from on High, The (Luke 1:78), 79
Dear Son, God's (Colossians 1:13), 124
Deliverer, The (Romans 11:26), 110
Diadem of Beauty, A (Isaiah 28:5), 41
Door of the Sheep, The (John 10:7), 96

Elect, God's (Isaiah 42:1), 46
Emmanuel (Matthew 1:23), 65
Ensign of the People, An (Isaiah 11:10), 36
Eternal Life, That (1 John 1:2), 154
Everlasting Father, The (Isaiah 9:6), 33
Everlasting God, The (Isaiah 40:28), 45
Everlasting Light (Isaiah 60:20), 53
Everlasting Strength (Isaiah 26:4), 40
Excellent (Psalm 148:13), 24
Express Image of His Person, The (Hebrews
    1:3), 135

Faithful and True Witness, The (Revelation
    3:14), 162
Faithful Witness, The (Revelation 1:5), 157
Finisher of Our Faith, The (Hebrews 12:2), 147
First and the Last, The (Revelation 1:17), 159
First Begotten of the Dead, The (Revelation
    1:5), 157
Firstborn, God's (Psalm 89:27), 22
Firstborn Among Many Brethren, The (Romans
    8:29), 108
Firstborn from the Dead, The (Colossians
    1:18), 127

Firstborn of Every Creature, The (Colossians 1:15), 125

Firstfruits of Them that Sleep, The (1 Corinthians 15:20), 116

Forerunner, The (Hebrews 6:20), 140

Fortress, My (Psalm 18:2), 18

Foundation, The (1 Corinthians 3:11), 114

Friend of Sinners (Matthew 11:19), 67

Friend that Sticks Closer than a Brother, A (Proverbs 18:24), 24

Gift of God, The (John 4:10), 93

Glorious Throne, A (Isaiah 22:23), 38

Glory, My (Psalm 3:3), 17

Glory of God's People Israel, The (Luke 2:32), 82

God (Hebrews 1:8), 136

God Blessed Forever (Romans 9:5), 109

God Manifest in the Flesh (1 Timothy 3:16), 131

God My Saviour (Luke 1:47), 78

God of the Whole Earth, The (Isaiah 54:5), 50

Good Master (Mark 10:17), 74

Good Shepherd, The (John 10:11), 96

Governor, A (Matthew 2:6), 66

Grain of Wheat, A (John 12:23–24), 97

Great God, The (Titus 2:13), 134

Great High Priest, The (Hebrews 4:14), 139

Great Light, A (Isaiah 9:2), 31

Great Prophet, A (Luke 7:16), 85

Great Shepherd of the Sheep, The (Hebrews 13:20), 148

Guest, A (Luke 19:7), 86

He that Filleth All in All (Ephesians 1:23), 120

He that Lives (Revelation 1:18), 160
He that Shall Come (Hebrews 10:36–37), 145
Head, The (Ephesians 4:15), 122
Head of Every Man, The (1 Corinthians 11:3), 116
Head of the Body, The (Colossians 1:18), 126
Head over All Things (Ephesians 1:22), 120
Head Stone of the Corner, The (Psalm 118:22), 23
Heir of All Things (Hebrews 1:2), 134
Helper, My (Hebrews 13:6), 148
Hidden Manna, The (Revelation 2:17), 161
Hiding Place from the Wind, A (Isaiah 32:2), 42
High Tower, My (Psalm 144:2), 23
Higher than the Heavens (Hebrews 7:26), 143
Him Whom My Soul Loveth (Song of Solomon 3:2), 27
Holy and True (Revelation 6:10), 164
Holy Child Jesus, God's (Acts 4:27), 104
Holy One, God's (Acts 2:27), 103
Holy One of God, The (Mark 1:24), 72
Holy One of Israel, The (Isaiah 49:7), 47
Hope, Our (1 Timothy 1:1), 130
Hope of Glory (Colossians 1:27), 128
Hope of His People, The (Joel 3:16), 59
Hope of Israel, The (Jeremiah 14:8), 55
Horn of Salvation (Luke 1:69), 78
Husband, Thine (Isaiah 54:5), 50

I Am (John 8:58), 95
Image of God, The (2 Corinthians 4:4), 118
Image of the Invisible God, The (Colossians 1:15), 125
Intercessor, Our (Hebrews 7:25), 142

Jehovah (Isaiah 40:3), 36
Jesus (Matthew 1:21), 65
Jesus Christ the Righteous (1 John 2:1), 155
Jesus of Nazareth (Acts 22:8), 107
Jesus the Christ (Matthew 16:20), 70
Judge of the Quick and the Dead (2 Timothy
    4:1–2), 132
Just One, The (Acts 7:52), 105

Keeper, Our (John 17:12), 101
King, The (Zechariah 14:16), 61
King in His Beauty, The (Isaiah 33:17), 44
King of Glory (Psalm 24:10), 20
King of Israel, The (John 1:49), 92
King of Kings (Revelation 17:14), 166
King of Peace (Hebrews 7:2), 141
King of Righteousness (Hebrews 7:2), 141
King of Saints (Revelation 15:3), 165
King of the Jews, The (Mark 15:2), 77
King over All the Earth (Zechariah 14:4–9), 61
King's Son, The (Psalm 72:1), 22

Lamb in the Midst of the Throne, The (Revela-
    tion 7:17), 164
Lamb of God, The (John 1:29), 90
Lamb Slain, The (Revelation 13:8), 165
Lamb Without Blemish or Spot, A (1 Peter
    1:19), 149
Last Adam, The (1 Corinthians 15:45), 117
Lawgiver, Our (Isaiah 33:22), 44
Leader, A (Isaiah 55:4), 51
Life, The (John 14:6), 99
Lifter up of Mine Head, The (Psalm 3:3), 17
Light of Israel, The (Isaiah 10:17), 34
Light of Men, The (John 1:4), 89

Light of the City, The (Revelation 21:23), 168
Light of the Gentiles, A (Isaiah 42:6), 46
Light of the Morning, The (2 Samuel 23:4), 15
Light of the World, The (John 8:12), 95
Light to Lighten the Gentiles, A (Luke 2:32), 82
Lily of the Valleys, The (Song of Solomon 2:1), 27
Lion of the Tribe of Judah, The (Revelation 5:5), 163
Living Stone, A (1 Peter 2:4), 150
Lord, The (Romans 10:13), 109
Lord and My God, My (John 20:28), 102
Lord Both of the Dead and the Living (Romans 14:9), 110
Lord from Heaven, The (1 Corinthians 15:47), 118
Lord God, The (Isaiah 40:10), 45
Lord God Omnipotent (Revelation 19:6), 167
Lord Jesus (Acts 7:59), 106
Lord Mighty in Battle, The (Psalm 24:8), 19
Lord of All (Acts 10:36), 106
Lord of Glory, The (1 Corinthians 2:8), 114
Lord of Hosts, The (Isaiah 6:3), 29
Lord of Lords (Revelation 17:14), 166
Lord of Peace (2 Thessalonians 3:16), 129
Lord of the Sabbath (Luke 6:5), 84

Maker, My (Isaiah 54:5), 49
Man, The (John 19:5), 102
Man Approved of God, A (Acts 2:22), 103
Man Christ Jesus, The (1 Timothy 2:5), 131
Man of Sorrows, A (Isaiah 53:3), 48
Man Whom He Has Ordained, That (Acts 17:31), 107
Master (John 13:13), 98

Master of the House, The (Luke 13:25), 86
Mediator, The (1 Timothy 2:5), 130
Mediator of a Better Covenant (Hebrews 8:6), 144
Mediator of the New Covenant (Hebrews 12:24), 147
Messenger of the Covenant, The (Malachi 3:1), 62
Messiah (John 4:25), 93
Mighty God, The (Isaiah 9:6), 32
Minister of the Circumcision (Romans 15:8), 111
Minister of the Sanctuary (Hebrews 8:2), 144
Morning Star, The (Revelation 2:28), 160

Nail in a Sure Place, A (Isaiah 22:23), 37
Nazarene (Matthew 2:23), 67
Nobleman, A (Luke 19:12), 87

Offering, An (Ephesians 5:2), 122
Offspring of David, The (Revelation 22:16), 169
Ointment Poured Forth (Song of Solomon 1:3), 25
One Lord (Ephesians 4:5), 121
One Son, His Wellbeloved (Mark 12:6), 76
Only Begotten of the Father, The (John 1:14), 90
Only Begotten Son, God's (John 3:16), 92
Overcomer, The (John 16:33), 100
Own Son, God's (Romans 8:32), 108

Passover, Our (1 Corinthians 5:7), 115
Peace, Our (Ephesians 2:14), 121
Peace Offering, The (Leviticus 3:1), 13
Physician (Luke 4:23), 84

Plant of Renown, A (Ezekiel 34:29), 57
Polished Shaft, A (Isaiah 49:2), 47
Portion of Jacob, The (Jeremiah 10:16), 55
Potter, Our (Isaiah 64:8), 54
Power of God, The (1 Corinthians 1:24), 111
Priest Forever, A (Hebrews 5:6), 139
Prince and a Saviour, A (Acts 5:30–31), 105
Prince of Life, The (Acts 3:15), 104
Prince of Peace, The (Isaiah 9:6), 33
Prince of Princes, The (Daniel 8:25), 58
Prince of the Kings of the Earth, The (Revelation 1:5), 158
Prophet Mighty in Deed and Word, A (Luke 24:19), 88
Prophet of Nazareth, The (Matthew 21:11), 71
Prophet of the Highest, The (Luke 1:76), 79
Purifier (Malachi 3:3), 63

Quickening Spirit, A (1 Corinthians 15:45), 117

Rabbi (John 1:49), 91
Ransom, A (Mark 10:45), 75
Redeemer, The (Isaiah 59:20), 52
Redemption (1 Corinthians 1:30), 113
Refiner (Malachi 3:3), 62
Refuge from the Storm, A (Isaiah 25:4), 39
Restingplace (Jeremiah 50:6), 56
Restorer (Psalm 23:3), 19
Resurrection, The (John 11:25), 97
Rewarder, A (Hebrews 11:6), 146
Righteous Branch, A (Jeremiah 23:5), 56
Righteous Judge, The (2 Timothy 4:8), 133
Righteous Servant, God's (Isaiah 53:11), 49
Righteousness (1 Corinthians 1:30), 112
Rivers of Water in a Dry Place (Isaiah 32:2), 43

Rock of My Salvation, The (2 Samuel 22:47), 15
Rock of Offence, A (1 Peter 2:7–8), 151
Rod out of the Stem of Jesse, A (Isaiah 11:1),
    34
Root of David, The (Revelation 5:5), 163
Root of Jesse, A (Isaiah 11:10), 35
Root out of a Dry Ground, A (Isaiah 53:2), 48
Rose of Sharon (Song of Solomon 2:1), 26
Ruler, A (Micah 5:2), 59

Sacrifice to God, A (Ephesians 5:2), 123
Salvation of God, The (Luke 2:30), 81
Sanctification (1 Corinthians 1:30), 113
Sanctuary, A (Isaiah 8:14), 30
Saviour of the World, The (1 John 4:14), 155
Sceptre, A (Numbers 24:17), 14
Seed of Abraham, The (Hebrews 2:16), 137
Seed of the Woman, The (Genesis 3:15), 11
Sent of the Father, The (John 17:18), 101
Separate from Sinners (Hebrews 7:26), 143
Servant, A (Philippians 2:7), 124
Servant, God's (Matthew 12:18), 68
Shadow from the Heat, A (Isaiah 25:4), 39
Shadow of a Great Rock in a Weary Land (Isa-
    iah 32:2), 43
Shepherd, My (Psalm 23:1), 18
Shield, My (Psalm 3:3), 16
Shiloh (Peacemaker) (Genesis 49:10), 12
Sign, A (Luke 2:34), 83
Son of Abraham (Matthew 1:1), 64
Son of David, The (Matthew 1:1), 64
Son of God, The (John 1:34), 91
Son of Man, The (Mark 10:33), 75
Son of Mary, The (Mark 6:3), 74
Son of the Father, The (2 John 3), 156

Son of the Highest, The (Luke 1:32), 77
Son of the Living God, The (Matthew 16:16), 69
Son of the Most High God (Mark 5:7), 73
Sower, A (Matthew 13:37), 69
Spiritual Rock, That (1 Corinthians 10:4), 115
Star, A (Numbers 24:17), 13
Stone Cut Without Hands (Daniel 2:34–5), 57
Stone of Israel, The (Genesis 49:24), 12
Stone of Stumbling, A (1 Peter 2:7–8), 151
Stranger and an Alien, A (Psalm 69:8), 21
Strength and My Song, My (Isaiah 12:2), 37
Strength to the Poor (Isaiah 25:4), 38
Strong Hold, A (Nahum 1:7), 60
Strong Rock, My (Psalm 31:2), 20
Strong Tower, A (Psalm 61:3), 21
Sun of Righteousness, The (Malachi 4:2), 63
Sure Foundation, A (Isaiah 28:16), 41
Surety of a Better Testament (Hebrews 7:22),
    142
Sweetsmelling Savour, A (Ephesians 5:2), 123

Temple, The (Revelation 21:22), 168
Testator, The (Hebrews 9:16), 145
Testifier, The (Revelation 22:20), 170
That Worthy Name (James 2:7), 149
Tried Stone, A (Isaiah 28:16), 42
True God, The (1 John 5:20), 156
True Light, The (John 1:9), 89
Truth, The (John 14:6), 99

Unspeakable Gift, God's (2 Corinthians 9:15),
    119
Upholder of All Things, The (Hebrews 1:3),
    136

Vine, The (John 15:5), 100

Wall of Fire, A (Zechariah 2:5), 60
Way, The (John 14:6), 98
Wisdom of God, The (1 Corinthians 1:24),
    112
Witness to the People, A (Isaiah 55:4), 51
Wonderful (Isaiah 9:6), 31
Word, The (John 1:1), 88
Word of God (Revelation 19:13), 167
Word of Life, The (1 John 1:1), 153

Young Child, The (Matthew 2:9), 66